ENDU[illegible]
THE H[illegible]

CW01637198

A British Soldier in Palestine, 1946–1947

Trevor Hall

(Royal Artillery, 1945–48)

ARCTURUS PRESS

2005

© Trevor Hall, 2005

The right of Trevor Hall to be identified as the author of this book is hereby asserted by him in accordance with the Copyright Designs and Patents Act 1988.
All rights reserved. No part of this publication may be recorded, reproduced, stored in a retrieval system or transmitted in any form or by any means electrical, electronic, mechanical or otherwise, without the written consent of the Author.

ISBN 0 907322 92 1

Published by
Arcturus Press
The Manse : Fleet Hargate : Lincolnshire PE12 9LL : England

Phone 01406 423971 : Fax 01406 422191

Contents

Illustrations

San Dimitrio, an unseaworthy ship carrying illegal immigrants, in Haifa harbour, 1946

Introduction

Both I and the proprietor of Arcturus Press, publishers of this book, served in the British Army in Palestine during the closing years of the League of Nations Mandate authorising Britain to govern that strife-ridden land after it had been liberated from Turkish rule by a joint British-Anzac force under General Allenby in 1917–18. In 1945, one of the consequences of the defeat of Germany in the west by US, British and Canadian forces, (supported by units composed of escapees from all the German-occupied nations of Europe), and in the east by the armies of the USSR, was that thousands of Jewish prisoners were liberated from the infamous Nazi concentration camps; and having no wish to return to their former homes, started to pour into Palestine in a huge wave of uncontrolled immigration. One cannot but have enormous sympathy for them; but at the same time, the rights of the existing Arab Muslim population had to be respected as well. After all, Muslim soldiers from India had played no small part in the defeat of the Germans in North Africa, and the part played by Arab guerrillas in the liberation of Palestine in 1917–18 was a substantial contribution to victory then, too.

Whatever the rights and wrongs of the situation, the British Government, as holders of the League of Nations Mandate, and therefore answerable to the League for the maintenance of law and order in Palestine, attempted to control the huge flow of immigrants which, quite apart from anything else, was putting a considerable strain on the infrastructure of the country. Needless to say, it was the British Army and the Palestine Police who had to pull the politician's chestnuts out of the fire and do the best they could in what was, with hindsight, a no-win situation. In so doing, they annoyed the indigenous Muslim inhabitants for letting in what they considered to be too many Jews, and stoked up even greater hatred among certain elements of the Jewish population for not letting in enough!

I was called up in February 1945 and did not leave England until after WW2 was over. In Palestine there were still many British soldiers who had helped to free thousands of the inmates of the concentration camps, and neither they nor we latecomers (including National Servicemen) were too pleased to be spat on and called "British Nazi bastards", or even filthier names, when carrying out our orders in Palestine.

I do not believe that this abuse was really condoned by many of the Jews in Palestine at the time, whether indigenous or post-war immigrant, but as the function of terrorists the world over is to terrorise not only those they deem their enemies but also those of their own side whose support they consider to be insufficiently enthusiastic, they are able to exert an influence quite disproportionate to their actual numbers.

Some years ago, I saw a couple of lines of poetry written by Sir John Harington in the time of the first Queen Elizabeth. It runs:

Treason doth never prosper, what's the reason?
For if it prosper, none dare call it treason.

If we substitute "terror" for "treason," we have the course of much modern history in a nutshell.

When I think of our time in the Holy Land I recall that when danger threatened, some would kiss the photo of a loved one, or finger a medal or a keepsake Others crossed themselves or "touched wood." When danger came too swiftly to invoke the aid of such talismans, we could only hold to our beliefs, our faith that some Higher Power was on our side.

For almost sixty years I have never mentioned that personage whom I saw from time to time in the Holy Land, but who was not seen by anyone else who happened to be with me. My name for him was The Galilean; and to this day he stays in my mind as one whose appearances I cannot attribute to coincidence, imagination or fever-induced hallucination.

So my time in the Holy Land was influenced in three ways; firstly, by doing my military duty and trying to stay alive; secondly, keeping sane by thinking about my family and home in one of England's most beautiful places, the Peak district; and thirdly, by the intervention of that mysterious figure whom I have just described, but am quite unable to explain. All I can do is to quote another two lines of poetry, this time by William Cowper:

God moves in a mysterious way
His wonders to perform.

Finally, the title of this book was suggested by yet more poetry, this time a line from A E Housman :

Let us endure an hour and see injustice done.
(A Shropshire Lad, XLVIII)

Who were the real victims of injustice in post-war Palestine, readers must judge for themselves.

Trevor Hall, Buxton, May 2005

Prologue I

Before starting my story, I reproduce below, a couple of typical examples of anti-British propaganda which were circulated in Palestine, 1945–1948. I make no comment – they speak for themselves.

THE VOICE OF FIGHTING ZION
THE BROADCASTING STATION OF THE NATIONAL MILITARY ORGANISATION IN PALESTINE.
BROADCAST 11 AUGUST 1946

A BLOCKADE – IMPOSED ON LAND AND SEA – IS THE TRADITIONAL WEAPON OF BRITAIN. SHE USED IT AGAINST LITTLE HOLLAND; SHE USED IT AGAINST THE AMERICAN REVOLUTIONARIES; SHE USED IT DURING THE LONG DRAWN OUT CAMPAIGN AGAINST NAPOLEON AND SHE CONTINUED TO USE IT DURING BOTH WORLD WARS. NOW BRITAIN HAS RESORTED TO THE BLOCKADE AS A WEAPON OF WAR AGAINST THE JEWISH NATION.

BUT INASMUCH AS THE WAR AGAINST THE PERSECUTED NATION OF ISRAEL HAS NO EQUAL IN THE HISTORY OF WARFARE, THE ANTI-JEWISH BLOCKADE HAS NOTHING SIMILAR TO IT IN THE REALMS OF SATANIC BARBARITY. IN FORMER WARS BLOCKADES WERE DIRECTED MAINLY AGAINST TRADE, RAW MATERIALS, WARLIKE EQUIPMENT, ARMS AND AMMUNITION. HOWEVER, THE ANTI-JEWISH BLOCKADE WHICH IS IMPOSED IS INTENDED TO BE APPLIED DIRECTLY AGAINST PEOPLE. BUT WHAT PEOPLE! THERE ARE THOSE WHO CAME OUT OF THE DEATH CAMPS; THOSE WHO FOR A PERIOD OF SIX YEARS SUFFERED IN HELL; THOSE WHOSE LIVES EXPERIENCED POGROMS AND BLOODSHED; THOSE WHO HAVE NEITHER MOTHER, FATHER, SISTER NOR BROTHER; THOSE WHO HAVE NOTHING LEFT IN LIFE BUT THE HOMELAND WHICH HAS TO TAKE THE PLACE OF MOTHER, FATHER, SISTER AND BROTHER IN THEIR LIVES; THAT MUST BRING BACK SOME REASON AND PURPOSE IN THEIR LIVES. AGAINST SUCH PEOPLE AS THESE, THE TREACHEROUS BRITISH SAW FIT TO UNFURL THE NETWORK OF BLOCKADE ON SEA AND LAND; AGAINST PEOPLE SUCH AS THESE ACCURSED BRITAIN CLOSED THE ONLY ROAD TO SALVATION. WAS THERE EVER CRUELTY SUCH AS THIS? WAS THERE EVER A BLOCKADE SUCH AS THIS? WAS THERE EVER SUCH A CRIME AS THIS? WAS THERE, AFTER HITLER AND HIMMLER, AFTER PREMEDITATED MASS MURDER, WAS THERE EVER SUCH A MURDER OF THE MASSES?

OF COURSE, THE BLOCKADE IS ONLY ONE TYPE OF WARFARE THAT THE EVIL EMPIRE EMPLOYS AGAINST OUR PEOPLE. BRITAIN IN HER CAMPAIGN OF ANTI-JEWISH DESTRUCTION USES MANY MEANS. SHE USES NAZI SUPPRESSION, THE FORCE OF INTIMIDATION, DIPLOMATIC MACHINATIONS AND SYSTEMATIC HUMILIATION, ALL OF WHICH HAVE BUT ONE PURPOSE, TO PUT AN END TO JEWISH ASPIRATIONS OF FREEDOM; TO REMOVE ISRAEL FROM THE REACH OF HER

SONS WHO ARE TRYING TO REACH ITS SHORES WITH ALL THEIR STRENGTH AND THE REMAINDER OF THEIR HOLY SCROLLS, AND TO IMPRISON US IN A GHETTO AND FINALLY HAVE DOMINION OVER OUR PLUNDERED LAND.

THEN THE PROGRAMME WOULD BE ANNOUNCED BY THE TREACHEROUS LIQUIDATORS: "THE PLAN OF FEDERALISATION FOR PALESTINE." THIS PLAN GIVES THE DESTRUCTIVE BRITISH EVERYTHING THAT THEY DESIRE, UNLIMITED SOVEREIGNTY OVER OUR LAND: A JEWISH GHETTO THE AREA AND POPULATION OF WHICH WOULD BE THE SAME AS THE WARSAW GHETTO AND WHOSE FATE WOULD BE THE SAME. INASMUCH AS THE GERMAN NAZIS PREFERRED TO ACHIEVE THEIR AIM WITH THE ASSISTANCE OF THE JEWS THEMSELVES, SO THE BRITISH NAZIS ARE TRYING TO IMPLEMENT THEIR SATANIC PROGRAMME BY "COOPERATION" WITH A JEWISH "COUNCIL OF ELDERS," EITHER THIS ONE OR ANOTHER. WHY SHOULD THERE BE WARS? WHY OPPOSITION? WHY SHOULD THERE BE BRITISH VICTIMS? WHY INTERNATIONAL INVOLVEMENT? WHY A BLOODY CAMPAIGN? WHY SHOULD THERE BE ALL OF THESE IF IT IS POSSIBLE TO OBTAIN THE AGREEMENT OF CERTAIN JEWISH CIRCLES TO THE PROGRAMME OF LIQUIDATION?

FURTHERMORE, TO OBTAIN THEIR AGREEMENT, THE DESTRUCTIVE BRITISH ARE AGAIN EMPLOYING TWO BRILLIANT NAZI TACTICS: FEAR, LIKE CONFRONTING A HIGHWAY ROBBER. DO YOU UNDERSTAND THE GAOLERS OF 100,000 PRISONERS OF THE CAMPS? – WITH A REVOLVER POINTED STRAIGHT AT THE FOREHEAD – "SIGN THIS PROGRAMME OF OURS AND ENTER THE GHETTO OF YOUR OWN FREE WILL. . . " SOMETHING ELSE . . . (INDEED IT IS POSSIBLE TO SAY WITH CERTAINTY THAT EVEN IF THE BRITISH WEREN'T ALLOWING IN 10,000 JEWS, THEY STILL HAVE A WEAPON IN THEIR HANDS AGAINST THE INNOCENT . . .) THAT IS THE IMPLICATION BEHIND THE MORRISON LEGISLATION THAT HE HAS LAID BEFORE PARLIAMENT. ONE SHOULD VIEW THIS IN ITS ENTIRETY, I.E. THEORETICAL BRITISH AGREEMENT TO THE IMMIGRATION OF 100,000 ON CONDITION THAT THERE IS EXPLICIT JEWISH AGREEMENT TO WAIVE THE CLAIM TO PALESTINE AND TO ESTABLISH A GHETTO LIKE A GRAVE. LIKE A GRAVE, NOT ONLY FOR THE HOPES OF A SUBJUGATED NATION, BUT ALSO FOR ITS LIVING SONS.

THE SECOND TACTIC, ALSO OF A NAZI TYPE; ENHANCING THE PRESTIGE – IN THE EYES OF THE JEWS – OF QUISLINGS OR THOSE ESTABLISHED AS THE SUPPORTERS OF QUISLINGS, THE EDITOR OF THE NEWSPAPER "HA-ARETZ" WAS SUDDENLY CALLED "A SHINING BEACON" AND EVEN THAT OLD FOX CHURCHILL, WHO CLAIMS THAT HE NEVER KNEW ANYTHING ABOUT THE EXTERMINATION OF MILLIONS IN EUROPE; CHURCHILL, WHO WAS PRIVY TO MORE INFORMATION THAN ANY OTHER PERSON DURING WORLD WAR TWO; CHURCHILL, WHO STRESSED THAT IT WAS IMPOSSIBLE FOR THE REMNANTS OF THE JEWS IN EUROPE TO ENTER PALESTINE; CHURCHILL, WHO CRITICISED THE

LABOUR GOVERNMENT, NOT BECAUSE IT WAS DESTROYING THE JEWISH ASPIRATIONS TO FREEDOM, BUT BECAUSE IT WAS DOING THIS UNTHINKINGLY – WITH THE VULGARITY OF BEVIN – WITHOUT APPEARANCE OF FRIENDSHIP – THIS CHURCHILL WHO DOES NOT FORGET TO SPEAK FLATTERINGLY ABOUT DR WEITZMAN IN A SARCASTIC TONE, SAYING OPENLY "WE WANTED THE JEWS TO KNOW THAT MANY IN THIS COUNTRY RESPECT DR WEITZMAN." IN LISTENING TO THESE WORDS AND ALSO TO THOSE OF LORD CRANBOURNE, WHO WAS FULSOME IN HIS PRAISE OF "ONE OF THE GREATEST MEN OF OUR TIME," WE HEAR AGAIN THE WORDS OF HITLER AND OF EVENTS IN OCCUPIED PARIS ABOUT THE GREAT OLD MARSHAL WHO WAS SENT BY DIVINE PROVIDENCE TO SAVE FRANCE . . .

THAT THEN IS THE POSITION. A TRAGIC SITUATION, A DANGEROUS SITUATION, A SITUATION THAT IN ESSENCE THREATENS THE SURVIVAL OF THE NATION. HOWEVER, THERE IS A POSITIVE ASPECT TO ALL: IT IS CLEAR, SO CLEAR AS TO BE WITHOUT A SHADOW OF A DOUBT, CLEAR TO EVERY PERSON IN ISRAEL WHO HAS EXPERIENCED A BLOODY EVENT AND WHO NOW HAS A CHOICE, FOR THOSE WHO STAND TODAY IN THEIR OWN LAND OR IN THE COUNTRIES OF THE DIASPORA. THE CHOICES ARE SIMPLE, FRIGHTENING AND GREAT IN THEIR SIMPLICITY AND THEY CANNOT BE EVADED:

EITHER A WAR OF LIBERATION OR IMPRISONMENT WITH TREACHERY
EITHER A FREE HOMELAND OR A GHETTO
EITHER A POPULAR UPRISING OR PROLONGED DEATH THROES
EITHER A JEWISH ARMY FIGHTING AND FREE OR "ILLEGAL TERRORISTS"
EITHER A JEWISH GOVERNMENT OR A SCHOLAR OF GREAT KNOWLEDGE

WITH OUR KNOWLEDGE OF THIS GENERATION, THIS GENERATION THAT HAS SEEN WITH ITS OWN EYES OR WITH THE EYES OF ITS SOUL THE SMOKE OF THE CREMATORIA AT TREBLINKA, THE GENERATION THAT HAS INHERITED ALL THE SACRIFICES OF GOD'S TEMPLES AND ALL THE HEROISM OF THE JEWISH FREEDOM FIGHTERS–WE KNOW WHAT THIS GENERATION WILL CHOOSE. THEREFORE, BE AFRAID, YOU DESTRUCTIVE BRITISH. YOU HAVE FELT PAIN AND WILL FEEL MORE, NOT ONLY IN THE LAND WHICH IS BESIEGED, BUT IN THE FOUR CORNERS OF THE EARTH AS THE OUTSTRETCHED ARM OF THE HEBREW SOLDIER WILL FIGHT YOU, AS YOU FOUGHT HIS UNFORTUNATE COUNTRY : WITHOUT MERCY.

WE SEE THE FRONT IN ITS ENTIRETY
BROADCAST ON WEDNESDAY 14 AUGUST 1946

THE ARMY OF LIBERATION IS SILENT IN MEMORY OF THE JEWISH SOLDIERS WHO FELL LAST NIGHT IN HAIFA AT THE HANDS OF THE MURDEROUS BRITISH. THEIR BLOOD, WHICH WAS SPILT FOR THE SAKE OF BROTHERS WISHING TO RETURN TO THEIR HOMELAND, WILL BE AS THE BLOOD OF THE FIGHTING HEROES – A CEMENT WHICH WILL UNIFY AND BIND THE NATION, WHEREVER IT

IS, AND CAUSE IT TO STAND AS A LIVING SHIELD BEHIND THE FAÇADE OF WAR. THIS PURE AND HOLY BLOOD WILL NOT BE FORGOTTEN, NOR WILL THE DESTRUCTIVE BRITISH BE FORGIVEN. IT WILL BE ENTERED IN THE NEVER-ENDING ACCOUNT OF BLOOD WRITTEN BY THE HANDS OF THOSE DESPOILERS OF OUR HOMELAND, BETWEEN THE NATION OF ISRAEL AND ITS MERCILESS OPPRESSORS. MAY GOD CURSE THEM AND SEEK JUSTICE.

WE HAVE REACHED THIS STAGE. IN FRONT OF OUR EYES IS THE UNFORGETTABLE NIGHT OF DISASTER, DURING WHICH THE IMMIGRANTS ON BOARD "ATLANTIC" AND "SALVADOR" WERE DRIVEN OUT, AN EXPULSION WHICH SEALED THE FATE OF HUNDREDS OF THOUSANDS OF JEWS BECAUSE 11 BLOCKED THEIR SOLE PATH TO DELIVERANCE, AND WHEN HITLER WAS DESTROYING EUROPEAN JEWRY WITH HIS SLAUGHTER, HE WAS CARRYING OUT BRITAIN'S WISH. NOW HERE WE STAND AGAINST THE MURDEROUS BRITISH WHO HAVE THE SAME AIM: THE DESTRUCTION OF THE JEWISH NATION, THE DESTRUCTION OF THE NATION THAT CLAIMS OWNERSHIP TO PALESTINE BECAUSE THEY HAVE DECIDED TO STEAL IT THEMSELVES. HERE, NOW, THE BRITISH CRIMINALS ARE EMPLOYING THE SAME BARBARIC METHODS, STRIKING THE BACKS OF IMMIGRANTS WITH RIFLE BUTTS, DRAGGING MEN, WOMEN AND CHILDREN BY THE HAIR, INJURING THEM UNTIL BLOOD FLOWED, THROWING THEM INTO FLOATING PRISONS. AGAIN THEY WERE THROWN AS SLAVES INTO DUNGEONS IN A LAND OF EXILE; IN A STRANGE LAND. AGAIN IT WAS DECREED THAT THEY SHOULD BE PRISONERS IN A STRANGE LAND AND THEN THE CRIMINAL HAND OF TREACHEROUS BRITAIN REACHED OUT. THE OCCUPYING GOVERNMENT DECLARED OPENLY THAT THAT WAS HOW EVERY JEW WOULD BE TREATED WHO INTENDED TO RISK THE GOVERNMENT'S LEGAL MURDER IN ORDER TO TRY TO REACH THE SHORES OF THE PLUNDERED HOMELAND. THUS A GREAT INSULT, INTENSE SUFFERING AND A GREAT WAVE OF WRATH, CARRIED ON A POWERFUL SEA BREAKS OVER THE WOUNDED NATION, WHETHER IN ZION OR THE DIASPORA.

BUT AFTER THE RAGE AT THEIR POSITION, AFTER THE BLOOD THAT BLED FROM OUR HEARTS AT THE DISGRACE OF THEIR BEING HUNTED AND DEPORTED, IT IS INCUMBENT ON US TO LOOK AT THE INNER LAW CONTAINED IN THESE EVENTS AND HOW THEY DEVELOP FROM A NECESSITY OF HISTORY; THE ANGLO-JEWISH WAR. THIS IS A WAR OF LIFE AND DEATH BETWEEN A FREEDOM-LOVING STATE AND BETWEEN OPPRESSION AND DESTRUCTION. THUS INDEED, ONLY THE FOOLISHLY STUPID, ONLY MISERABLE DEFEATISTS AND ISOLATED SHIRKERS ARE ABLE TO ASSUME OR–TO CLAIM THAT THEY ASSUME, THAT WHAT WILL BE, WILL BE. THE BRITISH "DEMOCRATS" WILL NOT RAISE A FINGER TO HELP THE JEWISH IMMIGRATION MOVEMENT. THOSE HYPOCRITES WITH THEIR AGREEMENT ON HYPOTHESES OF LACK OF MEANING PRODUCED THE THEORY OF (PRINT OBSCURED) ONE SECTION OF THE FRONT–TO A SECTION WHICH (PRINT OBSCURED) FROM THEIR KNOWLEDGE OF THE CENTRAL FRONT AND THE TRUE

PURPOSE. IN THEIR BLINDNESS THEY DID NOT SEE THAT THE DESTRUCTIVE BRITISH HAD PROHIBITED EVERYTHING AND THAT THEREFORE THERE COULD NEVER BE ANY REAL DEVELOPMENT OF THE NATION, NEITHER LEGALLY OR ILLEGALLY. HUMANITARIAN ARGUMENTS? CONSIDERATION OF PUBLIC OPINION/THESE STUPID PEOPLE FORGOT, OR THEY WANTED TO FORGET, THAT THOSE WHO SENT SIX MILLION JEWS TO THEIR DEATHS WOULD NOT REFRAIN FROM SENDING MANY MORE TO CONCENTRATION CAMPS IN ORDER TO ACHIEVE THEIR AIMS, THUS PUTTING THE BURIAL STONE ON THE RETURN TO ZION AND THE ASPIRATIONS OF JEWISH INDEPENDENCE.

TODAY, EVEN THIS FALSE HOPE HAS GONE. NOW IT IS CLEAR THAT A FRAGMENTED ARMY WILL NOT ACHIEVE ANY RESULT. IT IS NOW KNOWN THAT BEING SPECIFIC ABOUT THE ARMIES WHICH HAVE BEEN SET OUT IN STAGES WILL NOT MAKE IT ANY EASIER FOR THE POSITION OF THE NATION, BUT WILL PUT IT INTO DIRECT CONTACT WITH THE BRITISH POSITION: A "FEDERAL" GHETTO WHICH WILL BRING IT TO DESTRUCTION AND DEVASTATION. INDEED, A CRUEL SLAP IN THE FACE FOR THOSE "OPTIMISTS" AND HYPOCRITICAL DEFEATISTS, BUT THAT IS THE REAL CASE AND IS THE UNDERLYING RULE OF A WAR OF LIBERATION AND THERE IS NOT, AND NEVER WAS AND NEVER WILL BE ANY OTHER PATH.

THERE IS NO WAY OF AVOIDING THESE ISSUES AND ONE MUST INFER THAT FROM THE EVIDENCE OF THE UNCLOUDED SITUATION. THE CONCLUSIONS ARE THOSE THAT WE PROMULGATED SOME YEARS AGO, ON THE DAY THAT WE LAUNCHED OUR WAR OF DELIVERANCE. THE CONCLUSIONS ARE THOSE THAT WE REPEAT AND WILL CONTINUE TO REPEAT AT DAWN AND DUSK UNTIL IT SHALL BECOME THE PROPERTY OF EVERYONE AND ALL UNDERSTAND IT. NO "INDEPENDENT SECTORS" FOR THE FRONT. WE HAVE ONE FRONT ONLY. NO FRAGMENTED AIMS; WE HAVE ONE AIM ONLY. NO MOVEMENT IN STAGES; WE HAVE ONE WAR ONLY—TOTAL AND ON A WIDE SCALE. A WAR REQUIRES ITS PROSECUTION BY ALL MEANS, BY ALL METHODS AND IN ALL AREAS; A WAR WHOSE AIMS ARE TO TOPPLE THE OPPRESSIVE BRITISH ADMINISTRATION AND TO ESTABLISH IN ITS PLACE A FREE JEWISH GOVERNMENT THAT WILL REDEEM AND RESTORE THE LAND TO ITS SOUL. . . THEREFORE WE HAVE DEMANDED AND ARE NOW DEMANDING:-

NO GHETTO-LIKE, DEPENDENT, JUSTIFIED "ORGANISATIONS" SHOULD BE ESTABLISHED BUT A SOVEREIGN HEBREW GOVERNMENT ONLY, WITHIN AN INDEPENDENT FRAMEWORK THAT WILL CARRY ON THROUGH THE WAR TO INDEPENDENCE

NO CONTACTS TO BE ESTABLISHED WITH THE OCCUPYING REGIME BUT ALL RELATIONS WITH INSTITUTIONS AND REPRESENTATIVES SHOULD BE SEVERED.

NOT TO USE OUR FINANCE TO SET UP OPPRESSIVE INSTITUTIONS BUT TO ESTABLISH AN INDEPENDENT JEWISH TREASURY THAT WILL BE ABLE TO

SUPPLY THE NECESSITIES OF WAR.

NOT TO RAISE MILITARY OR DEFENSIVE ORGANISATIONS BUT TO ESTABLISH A UNIFIED HEBREW ARMY THAT FIGHTS AND LIBERATES.

NOT TO BE SATISFIED WITH SOLITARY WARLIKE ACTS OR "RETALIATORY" OR HIT-AND-RUN OPERATIONS BUT TO MAINTAIN A CONTINUOUS STATE OF WAR THAT WILL DEVELOP INTO A GENUINE UPRISING AND AN OVERPOWERING ASSAULT.

THAT IS THE POLITICO-MILITARY PROGRAMME: IT IS A PLAN FOR WAR: IT IS THE RIGHT PLAN FOR THE NATION WHICH IS BEING ENCIRCLED AND THREATENED WITH EXTINCTION AND WHICH HAS TWO ENEMIES: TREACHEROUS DESTRUCTIVE MURDER AND TIME; CURSED TIME. IN VIEW OF THIS THERE IS NO OTHER WAY FOR THE SALVATION OF THE NATION BUT THAT OF A DETERMINED WAR OF LIBERATION, WITH ALL ITS SACRIFICES AND UNCERTAINTIES.

DESPITE ALL THAT WE HAVE STRESSED BEFORE, IN ACCEPTING SUCH A POLICY AS THIS, WE SHALL MINIMISE THE NUMBER OF OUR CASUALTIES, WE SHALL INCREASE OUR HOPES AND BRING CLOSER THE DAY OF SURRENDER,, THE HOUR OF VICTORY THAT WILL SURELY COME.

CAPT. (RET) G.P. PORTMAN INT CORPS
(EX-2/B/SGT PALESTINE POLICE FORCE)

As I wrote earlier, no comment! T.H.

Prologue II

The Homecoming: January 14th 1948

No need for the 4 am call. I was awake and out of bed, the events of the past few hours already pushed to the back of my mind. By 0445 hours I had completed my ablutions, packed my kit and breakfasted like a King on porridge, fried eggs, bacon, beans and Spam.

Back in the tent my three fellow gunners were still fast asleep. The other two were on guard duties; on their empty beds I left both of them a parting gift of two bottles of beer. It was time to go. I took a last look at my "Rocket Troop" mates snoring and dreaming their dreams. 'Hursty' mumbled incoherently in his sleep – "Pooshlandithrum or whatever to you too, Hursty" I whispered back and slipped quietly out of the tent. Accompanied by the usual armed escort I left the 6th Field Royal Artillery Regimental area at 0500 hours. Minutes later we exited Camp 21.

On the open road the driver of the 15-cwt Bedford put his foot down on the throttle. We passed armoured cars, slow moving jeeps and foot patrols. Khaki shapes and blurred faces. Artillerymen, infantrymen and cavalry in their armour. Slow at crossroads, stop at checkpoint. White spearpoint sign of our own Div, and Pegasus of 6th Airborne. Watchful eyes from which youth has either fled or been stolen. Faces lined and tired. Pick up speed again, the roads are getting busier. REME, Ordnance and Service Corps going to and from their tasks. Royal Engineers and 'Signallers' with headphones on and 'Medics' rushing in a red-crossed Austin.

Palestine police and 'Redcaps' at the station. We came to a stop. I dismounted and gathered up my kit. "Take care, lads, and thanks for the ride!" "Good luck, Lofty, you jammy sod!" they shouted and set off back to the camp at Kfar Yona near Nathanya. I boarded the Haifa to Egypt train and joined five more in the compartment of the military carriage, six of us with things in common. We were all going home for demobilisation.

Six of us wearing the white triangle of the 1st British Infantry Division on our arms, sporting different cap badges but all of us had been carrying out the same duties. In six pairs of eyes a haunted look that came with time spent combating a merciless and virtually invisible foe.

So the mood was far from celebratory, for despite the vigilance of the patrols along the railway, the dangers from explosive devices and sniper's bullets were ever present.

Closer we came to the frontier. 'Clickety-clack', 'clickety-clack,' 'honour thy pledge', 'honour thy pledge', drummed the train. The brakes went on, the drumming slowed. Outside, British soldiers in khaki drill, Palestinians in clothes fashionable in biblical times. Like a rundown gramophone the iron wheels managed one last 'honour thy pledge' before coming to a halt with a clanking of buffers and a hiss of steam.

"I will," I said out loud. "Shalom", I heard a voice say. "Shalom", I replied.

To my embarrassment my travelling companions were looking at me wide-eyed as if waiting for an explanation. Thankfully the train gave a sudden jolt that caused all our immediate attention to be focused on falling kit bags and tin hats. Full speed ahead and the coming of the Sinai Desert. Blue skies and scorching sun coincided with a lightening of moods and a sense of great relaxation. As Palestine receded in the distance we knew at last we were really going home. Rifles were no longer at the ready but every rifle was still secure, for this is a country where everything not watched or tied down has a habit of disappearing.

Every time the train slowed or stopped it took on more non-paying roof passengers. In a window space wide open because of the stifling heat, the upside down grinning head of an Egyptian boy appeared.

"You buy dirty pictures?" "Eff off," said the Highlander opposite. "Awa' tha noo, cocky Jocky," the grinning head replied and disappeared rapidly upwards as the Highlander rose out of his seat. Presumably an accomplice on the roof of the carriage had hold of his ankles.

Good old Egypt with its people, colour, smells and the unusual. My last trip through the Sinai had been by road driving a 3-ton Bedford. Hurst, Herod and Bates were three of the armed escort; another was the photographer who took our photos, Knocker Hall, whose camera was always in action. Mid-journey we stopped for a break. Apart from a few distant rocks it was sand, endless sand. In places it had blown over and covered long stretches of the road. No signs of life in any direction. We had a drink of very warm water out of our water bottles, smoked and rested up for half an hour.

Three grubby faces looked down at us; the eldest of the Bedouin lads couldn't have been more than seven or eight years old. Outstretched hands twitched in time with their singsong requests for 'backsheesh' and cigarettes.

"Where the hell have you sprung from?" They grinned and pointed to the empty desert in the opposite direction to the distant rocks.

"English very good men, very good soldiers, you give backsheesh for our poor mother." "What's your name?" I asked the eldest who fascinated all of us with his eyes of sky blue and hair of bright ginger. "Backsheesh." I gave him a cigarette instead. "Backsheesh," he persisted, another cigarette changed hands. "That's your lot!" "Jimmy MacDoodle" he uttered in a Scottish brogue. "Sounds more Scottish that Bedouin!" "Och aye," he replied. "My father was a bloody good Scottish soldier."

We gave them their backsheesh and drove off, leaving them clutching their rewards of a few piastres and cigarettes and still pleading for more. A number of times in this land I had seen people appear like magic out of nowhere but never before or since have I seen a blue-eyed, ginger-haired, brown-skinned Bedouin.

It speaks volumes for the tutorial qualities of generations of British soldiers, that not only can most of the population of Egypt speak fluent English, but many can speak with a Scottish accent any kilt and sporran wearer would be proud of. Their ability to curse is remarkable and their range of swear words is second to none. However, it is noticeable that when they become over-excited (which is often), the swear words come out easily but often in the wrong order!

"Eggsanbread," "Eggsanbread." Before the train came to a halt we could hear him. Wearing a fez and carrying his wares on his shoulder he appeared at the open carriage window. "Eggsanbread and long live England."

"Eff off!" shouted the Highlander with such vehemence it made old "Eggsanbread" jump, which in turn caused a swarm of flies to rise in a buzzing cloud from the hard boiled eggs and slices of bread. Only the vendor knew what orifice the eggs had come from. They ranged in size from a quail's egg to something larger than a goose egg. Most were egg shaped but some were round and wobbly. With a grin and a flourish he brought the tray to the front of his chest, puffed out his cheeks and blew the flies away. He had our undivided attention. Briefly we saw the greyish white of the bread and the dullish greenish grey of the eggs before the return of the flies. As if by magic the tray now held what looked like over-curranted Eccles cakes and oval lumps of spotted dick. Old Eggsanbread swelled his cheeks, gave a puff, fluttered his hand and selected one of the smaller eggs. Holding it between thumb and forefinger he pursed his lips, made a loud kissing noise, opened his mouth and popped in the egg along with half a dozen flies. Rolling his eyes and giving little moans of pleasure, he chewed and swallowed with great relish. "Bloody good egg, plenty egg, plenty jig-a-jig," he said, making an obscene gesture. "You buy now, my friends!" "Eff off!" we shouted and busied ourselves swatting the infestation of flies he left behind.

Every time we slowed or stopped, vendors appeared in greater numbers and varieties as we neared our destination. Despite the heat, we kept the windows closed and watched them pass to and fro shouting their wares. Eggs and bread, coffee, honey sweet and black as the night, lemonade and orangeade, cakes of marzipan and sticky buns. With the crossing of the paths of 'Eggsanbread' and 'Stickeebuns,' dark halos rose over each tray and I watched with interest as more than a few flew from each swarm, changed places and settled down again.

Among their own people the vendors were doing a roaring trade. A quick check of my AB 64 revealed I had received two vaccinations and 14 inoculations against all manner of things including plague and cholera, but I wouldn't have trusted their protective qualities against even one toothful of that tray-borne food! Within the confined limits of my knowledge and experiences of salesmen, the likes of 'Eggsanbread' stand supreme!

156 Transit Camp at Port Said appeared to have changed little since I had passed through it when I first arrived in Egypt. We presented our documents and AB 64s at the office and having signed a couple of forms, were allocated sleeping quarters. With my five companions we were all together in the same tent.

It was only when drawing blankets and palliasse that I realised the Afrika Korps POWs who were working in the camp when I last passed through, had disappeared. "Where's the Jerry POWs?" I asked the bored-looking corporal taking signatures for the bedding. "Buggered off home, and we silly buggers are still stuck in this stinking hole!"

"Think yourself bloody lucky you're not stuck up in Palestine!" said a bloke from the 6th Airborne. The corporal coloured up and opened his mouth to say something and thought better of it.

After a meal and the luxury of a bath we were able to relax and settle down to a good nights' sleep, stress free, no guard duties, no patrols, no interruptions.

Next day I went through the presents I was taking home to my loved ones. Two 6-inch crucifixes inlaid with mother of pearl from Bethlehem. A small picture of a carpenter's workshop in Nazareth, a sprig of dried wild flowers from the Holy Land and a cigarette case. Fashioned from war debris aluminium, the cigarette case had the picture of a 'Spitfire' fighter plane engraved on the front. I had been in transit heading in the other direction when I purchased the case from its ingenious maker – an English-speaking Afrika Korps POW. We argued and after much bartering, 50 cigarettes got me the case. Like me, he was an artilleryman. "You anti-tank?" he asked. "No, field artillery, twenty-five pounders." He poked his chest, "Me, 88mm's, good"

"Very good gun," I agreed. I had never seen one myself but I'd heard plenty about them from some of the 'Desert Rats.' It was originally an anti-aircraft gun, capable of firing 20 high-velocity rounds a minute, and when used as an anti-tank gun firing armour-piercing ammunition, it was capable of knocking out any British tank.

Fritz was a collector of cap badges, As I was more than happy with the outcome of our bartering, I gave him my badge. "It's a spare, you can have it free." He was overjoyed, pointing to the inscription. "Tell me meaning, please," he asked. Speaking slowly while he wrote it down I told him "Everywhere Where Right and Glory Lead." "Because you my friend, I will make badge on case for nothing, come back in one hour." The case was awaiting me at the appointed time. On the back was engraved the badge of the Royal Artillery complete with the inscription – "UBIQUE QUO FAS ET GLORIA DUCUNT"

Confirming that the other four would keep an eye on our kits, 'Mac' the Highlander and myself went into Port Said. At intervals ever decreasing in time, 'Mac' shouted the same two words to the plethora of pimps, beggars, vendors of food, drink and dirty photos. Some of them grinned, some of them shouted the same two words back at us.

We stopped at a stall of colourful carpets, rugs and tapestries of all sizes. A tapestry caught my eye, just the thing to grace my mum's table or sideboard. An oasis, palm trees, camels and pyramids picked out in fine detail on a rich velvet soft background of deep red and edged with a golden fringe.

"General Monty, he buy carpet from me." "Eff off," said Mac. "You buy best carpet in Egypt, very cheap." "No," I said, fingering the tapestry I fancied. "Feel, very soft, bints work many weeks," moving his hand about as though using a needle and thread. "Much work, very fine."

I shook my head, "It's a machine made antimacassar! His eyes popped with indignation, "No mashin, not-" and he struggled in vain to get his tongue round antimacassar. "Bollocks," he said in the end with a large grin on his face.

When I offered him a tenth of his asking price his smile vanished. "You think me silly bugger?" he shouted. "No, I think you are a clever bugger whose prices are silly!" Half an hour had gone by. "Sod this," said Mac, "I'm going for a look round, see you back at camp, Lofty."

The bargaining continued; in a peculiar way we were both enjoying it. Several times I walked away and each time he shouted me back and reduced the price. In the end he called me a 'tight-arsed bugger.' I said "That's it, stuff your antimacassar, I'm off." He came after me again, but this time with the tapestry, which changed hands for the princely sum of one pound ten shillings. "You come back tomorrow, bring friends for bargains, tell them I bloody madman, I give things away." I shook my head "I'm sailing for home tomorrow." "You buy dirty pictures, very good?" Pictures, that's a good idea, I thought, but not the sort he and a multitude of others were selling.

I came across a combined gift shop and photographic studio which was most unusual, insofar as the prices were non-negotiable. All sorts of modern cameras were on display, a far cry from the box camera I'd known back home. Two booklets of pictures ranging from the ancient pyramids to modern Cairo, half a dozen picture postcards and a fez completed my shopping. Well satisfied with my purchases I returned to camp.

From on board ship I took a last look at Egypt. I thought of my mates in Palestine. I thought of comrades who would never come home. For four long days the Mediterranean shed its "calm as a millpond" mantle. It was a full-time occupation trying to hold on to the contents of my stomach. Sleep in the overcrowded and stuffy troop decks was the sleep of exhaustion.

With the easing of the storm my thoughts turned to the more pleasant things of life. There can be few nicer feelings than returning home from abroad after a lengthy spell of active service. If longer the active service, if greater the danger and the hardship, if further away from home make for a more enjoyable homecoming, then there must have been some already home and demobbed, whose homecoming must have been truly joyful. Throughout history, in two world wars and between and beyond, on land, on sea, in the air, in every theatre of conflict however remote or far flung, men from Tideswell in Derbyshire, my native village, served and still serve. Yet remarkably, Tideswell is a village of less than two thousand souls in total.

In Athens, 'Desert Rat' Joe Chapman and myself missed each other by a few hours. Joe would have been back at his home at the bottom of the 'Sawpit' for a year or more. No doubt he would have taken up work in the family joinery and undertaking business. Two Tideswell lads I did meet with, both in Palestine; Stan Walker who is eighteen months younger than me came out with the 17th/21st Lancers last year. The 'Death or Glory Boys' were patrolling the railway when we met up with each other. Patrols aren't static, so by necessity the meeting was brief. Stan told me the Lancers were off to Transjordan and then the Sudan. "Anywhere's better than Palestine," I told him. He nodded. "See you sometime, Trev."

"Take care, Stan." We parted and went our different ways.

Below deck the air became cooler as the ship cleared the Straits of Gibraltar and rolled its way into the Atlantic Ocean. I shook the creases out of my greatcoat, which apart from having its brass buttons polished once a week hadn't had an outing during daylight hours for a very long time. Leaving the blue and pungent haze of pipe and cigarette smoke, that hung heavy yet danced so lightly, I went up on deck. Buttoning up my greatcoat to the neck and pulling on my cap comforter, I sat down in a sheltered nook on the lee side of the ship. Even here and rugged up as I was, the bite of the wind chilled my bones. Within a short space of time the fuggy conditions below seemed a better option than those on deck. My hands turned blue, my nose was running. As they say back home, "It's an idle wind! It doesna goo round yer, it goos through yer!"

For dinner we had one of my favourite meals, corned beef hash and mashed potatoes followed by plum duff and custard. Raising my mug of tea I drank a silent toast to the ship's cooks.

During my time in the Army I could not recollect a week going by without corned beef and Spam popping their heads up in some concoction or other. Hot and cold, boiled and fried, plain and in batter at any time of the day, I never tire of it. I take my hat off to the Army Catering Corps. Thinking back to the time when we had no Christmas dinner thanks to our drunken cooks I'm inclined to put my hat back on again – but no, we survived. Bully beef and Spam in excess, a choice of two jams, bread as usual containing the extra protein of live weevils, lashings of tea and two bottles of beer. A repast fit for a King!

Thinking of cooks, where was that other Tideswellian, Ken Gilbert? Some months had gone by since I visited him in his cookhouse near Haifa. Ken was my age; we were at school together. Our demob groups were the same but we are not on the same draft.

No bands, just grey skies and cold rain greeted us when we disembarked at Liverpool. It was good to set foot on English soil again. No sign of 'Mac' when we boarded the train but we had said our goodbyes previously. Against orders, some had headed for the nearest pub and without doubt some missed the train.

Hardly a second glance from anyone for the boys in khaki; what a difference peace makes! It was understandable, for people had had a bellyful of war and its consequences and the rationing and the weather didn't help matters. For a fleeting moment I yearned for those times less than three years ago, when even strangers were shaking my hand, patting my back and buying me a beer.

In York the Army did me proud. I went in wearing a uniform of khaki and came out clad in a double breasted grey pinstripe suit, grey tie, grey trilby, grey socks and black shoes. Strange as it may seem so did the guardsman, the paratrooper, the signaller and half a dozen others. The only repeatable remark from those waiting to go in likened us to Al Capone's gang. We all promptly changed back into khaki for the journey home!

Bakewell, Hassop, Longstone and into the tunnel. I wiped the condensation from the carriage window and lit a 'Ship's Woodbine.' The burst into daylight came quicker than I anticipated. The 'clickety clack' of the train took on a different tone as it thundered on to the viaduct and into the countryside I know and love. Spectacular Monsal Dale, rearing hills all around, in places touching the scudding clouds.

Here and there a dry limestone wall picked out in greyish white. Large unequal portions of the grassy slope so close. Over on the other side the towering heights are topped in places by rocky outcrops with long skirts of scree held firm by dogrose, hawthorn and saplings of ash.

Also on the right and from Monsal Head receding with each 'clickety-clack,' the road tumbles down the Headstones hill and unfurls like a giant strap of liquorice along the green valley floor to brooding Cressbrook Mill. A fleeting glimpse of toy-like houses in tiers, perched high on steep slopes midst the dense woods of Cressbrook, eyecatching even in the drab bareness of a winter's day, a fairyland when flecked with snow.

Gone is the daylight and the 'clickety-clack' changes again as the express plunged into the tunnel's darkness. Daylight for a few seconds only, darkness and daylight. 'Clickety-clack' in fast changing tones. Litton Mill, riverside houses, old road by the brookside to Tideswell snaking away to the right. Open track, 'clickety-clack.' Meandering Wye and riverside road to Millers Dale. No more tunnels, just a cutting or two, worked out quarries on the left. Brakes go on 'clickety-clack' eases back and on the viaduct changes tone. River, road, corn mill and Railway Hotel down below. "Millers Dale! Millers Dale for Tideswell! Change for Buxton! Change for Buxton!"

Alighting from the carriage I looked towards Sid the porter to have a word or two, but he was busy helping someone off the train so I made for the exit. Was Jack Shaw still working in the railway goods shed? Had all the recipients of his lucky four-leaf clovers returned, I wondered?. Wilf Wood and Frank Swindell carried Jack's clovers over the seas and the oceans. Both served in the Royal Navy all through the war. Frank survived capture by the Germans and a long spell as a POW. Both are safely back home. Harry, the ticket clerk, asked me how I was. Before I could answer, the loud blast of a motor horn drew our attention. "Come on," I saw Juan mouthing and beckoning me to hurry up.

The express had been four and a half minutes late arriving and the driver of the blue and white bus was impatiently revving the engine.

"What's up, Juan?" I asked looking round the empty bus.

"Yer late in!" he shouted, looking over his shoulder and shoving the big knobbed gearstick forward, grating it into gear.

"Leave it there," he ordered as I attempted to pick my kit bag off the floor. With a lurch we set off. "Shut the door!" I slammed it to. "Yer look like breaking it," he said accusingly. Another lurch and I half fell and half sat in the seat across from him.

Cold as the interior of the bus was, the effort needed in getting a full lock on to negotiate the acute right hand bend out of the station yard brought beads of perspiration on the driver's forehead. Straightening it up and hauling it round a sharp left-handed bend a minute later caused the sweat to run.

Millers Dale church, the old Mill, the stream from Monks Dale and beyond. Rock Cottages and the steep old road to Tideswell rising on the left. Looking down on the backs and roofs of the 'Anglers Rest' and riverside houses to our right and we are into the long climb to the high ground.

I waited and waited for Juan to ask me about my Army service and where I'd been, but the only thing he talked about was the snow, fog and different sorts of ice of the Tideswell winter.

Ravenstor and the climb was accomplished. Now the pocket watch came out and was checked with the wrist watch which had been consulted several times since we set off. Unless things had altered while I'd been away, there was nothing to meet or catch at the end of the two and a half mile journey.

'Time is time' is Juan's motto. "Why was he late?"

"Who?"

"The London Manchester express of course!"

"How the hell do I know?"

"Where did you get on?"

"Derby."

"Was he late in Derby?"

"It was bang on time" I told him, although I didn't really know.

"Derby up to Millers Dale, I knew that's where he lost it," he said triumphantly. Silence while we negotiated the bends down towards the Plantation houses. Sniffing the air on the straight past the Filterbeds, I thought 'there's no change there.' A few minutes later came the smell of the gasworks. It was great to be back in Tideswell. Juan checked his watch with the clock on the 'Monkey House' and nodded.

"You've spent your time in the sun by the looks of yer." I didn't answer, my interest was in the large horse trough on the 'Jockey' hillock and the 'Horse and Jockey' pub behind, then we were in Cherry Tree Square.

"Think yourself lucky you've missed most of the winter."

For a moment he made me feel guilty as though I'd been on a holiday. I held my tongue.

"They've already had two 'Welcome Home' dinners, they won't be holding any more I can tell yer!"

"I don't give a bugger whether they do or they don't," I said heatedly, which brought a smile to his face.

"Are yer getting off at Chapmans?"

"No, George Hotel, I might as well get my money's worth!"

Into the Bank Corner I noticed the 'Griffin' still sat on the wall near the door of the District Bank. Past the Co-op where I worked prior to my call-up, Juan checked the time on the church clock with his watches. "It's a minute fast!"

"Well it's no good telling me."

"No, but I shall tell Tom Bagshaw when I see him!"

End of the line. I dismounted and shouldering my kit bag turned to Juan. "You'd be better off if you bought yourself a decent timepiece instead of those 'Mickey Mouse' watches."

"Goo on, ger off up inta th' Townyed wi yer!" he said with a twinkle in his eye.

Not a soul did I see until I neared my home. The little lad came running to meet me.

"How many Germans have yer shot, Trev?"

"Bloody thousands," I told him with a grin. Away went young Cecil Shirt, running home as fast as his legs could carry him and all the time shouting at the top of his voice. "Trev's shot bloody thousands of Germans!"

I shouldn't have said that I thought ruefully; after all, the only Germans I had seen were all prisoners of war. I opened the outer door and instinctively stamped on the broad brass strip fitted to prevent the prevailing west wind from blowing rainwater into the entry. Water shot up through the holes wetting my trouser leg. For the first time in my life I heard no shout of "Stop doing that, Trevor!"

My family were all waiting for me, Uncle Colin and Aunt Sarah came in from next door; it was good to be home. As always the kettle was singing on the hob. Before I sat down the tea was brewed and the pot fitted with its cosy. Not the usual 'Number 99' but the finest 'Indian Prince' Co-op tea, brewed with water from Tideswell reservoir. Water so hard, furring up everything from kettles to boilers. A mile it travels downhill, to most of the village, but the climb up into Townhead exhausts its pressure, so sometimes it just can't make it. Many believe that the water's properties are the cause of the large swelling in front of the throat known locally as 'Derbyshire Neck.' All are aware of the large numbers of various species of aquatic life usually referred to as 'wick things' that come through the tap, yet the tea it brews is sheer nectar.

"You look to have grown taller, Trevor!"

"I have, Mum," I replied and kicking my shoes off I stood straight with my back to the wall against the mark made by Uncle Joe a few days prior to my 18th birthday. 6' 1½ " read the measurement, 2" more than the mark of three years ago.

Re-united with my family, my sweetheart Stella and my friends. Enjoying mum's cooking and the comforts of home again. Sleeping soundly knowing the only alarm will not be one of danger but just the

Rhode Island Red cock crowing in Arnold's field behind. Thanks to the Army I now appreciated so many things that in the past I took for granted.

Now it's time to tell the story of how that appreciation came about.

The author at Kfar Yona, 1947

Chapter 1

Off to the Holy Land

In 1941 I was 14 and working and earning my keep. Later in the year Tideswell Home Guard accepted me into their ranks. Along with a few others who had no rifles or shotguns we were armed with pikes. Later I learned to shoot with the Canadian Ross rifle. During a week's course with the Army I learned as an Army cadet how to strip, assemble and fire the Bren light machine gun.

In February 1945 I received my Army call-up papers to report for infantry training at Lincoln.

It will always remain a source of wonderment to me, how the Army can take in thousands upon thousands of raw recruits and send them on six weeks later as disciplined soldiers. Everyone with a high standard of fitness, everyone able to kill with bullet, bomb, bayonet and bare hands. On top of that, all have been inoculated, vaccinated, made a will, had a hair cut and a 'short arm' inspection and teeth seen to.

By the time I got to France the war was over, with only the debris and scars remaining. On hard wooden seats with eight of us to a cramped compartment, we left Calais by train and arrived at Hyères in southern France the following day.

Two days later I sailed from Toulon to Piraeus. At Glyfada, a few miles southwest of Athens, I joined the Bengal Rocket Troop of the 1st Field Regiment of the Royal Artillery.

Poor Greece, as if she hadn't suffered enough under German occupation, now had warring factions amongst her own people. Many of the valiant Greek underground, our wartime allies, were now classed as terrorists. Such is the ease by which events and governments can turn friends into foes. We followed orders, did our best and became experienced in anti-terrorist duties.

In the autumn of 1946 we said goodbye to the 13th (Lucky Horseshoe) Division and Greece and sailed for Egypt. By way of Alexandria, Cairo, Port Said and the Sinai we arrived in Palestine and joined the 1st Infantry Division. Our base was at Ramat David, a few miles north of Nazareth. Over yonder, as I imagined it was in biblical times, was the white-robed Arab with his family and overburdened ass, his ox and patch of stony ground with water melons growing in the crooked shallow scrapes made by his wooden plough.

In the opposite direction, Palestine showed her modern face. The commune of Jewish settlers in shorts and skirts of denim blue with machinery that neither needed nor got any rest. Mighty tractors, implements of steel, sprinklers fed by water from deep bore holes, irrigate successive crops. Over there the ground is allowed no rest. Every slight breeze mingles a whiff of eucalyptus with the scent of orange blossom. Here and there, as if in exile from their groves, ancient olive trees with white-daubed trunks stood like sentinels. Among lush vegetation and in scorched desert scrub, wild flowers scattered and in drifts, bejewelled the ground and perfumed the air. It was indeed a land of milk and honey.

We were there in the role of peacekeepers. A few Danish lads served with us. Our numbers included a sprinkling of battle-hardened veterans, but for the most part we were teenaged conscripts. Some like myself had had an introduction to peacekeeping in Greece, but others were fresh out from Britain.

Tewfik, an Arab working in our camp told me his people would rejoice when we left his land. "When you are gone we will drive the Jews into the sea!" I shook my head, "I very much doubt it, they're getting support from many places including America and they grow stronger by the day."

There was no dialogue between ourselves and the Jews. They hated us for preventing boatloads of their people from entering Palestine illegally. Their hate was of an intensity I found it hard to comprehend. For us, life was a long monotonous round of guards and patrols. During the hours of darkness, only duties took us outside the barbed wire of the camp's perimeter. By necessity we were imprisoned by our own security, but it mattered little, for beyond our confines there was no joy, no laughter, no milk of human kindness in that Holy Land.

Not for the first time, politicians back home had given the British soldier a bed of nails to lie on and put him in a no-win situation.

"Any chance sir of taking eight of the off-duty men up to Tiberias for a swim in the lake?" The adjutant gave his permission and added, "Leave a list of your names at the Guardroom and be back by 1600."

With a kit bag full of oranges for sustenance we reached our destination. "So this is the 'Sea of Galilee,'" I said out loud looking down at water so clear I could see every pebble on the gentle sloping sea bed.

'They must be the Hills of Bashan mentioned in the Bible as causing violent storms,' I thought, looking eastwards at heights comparable to the highest in the Peak District back home.

I am no swimmer but I stripped off and had a quick dip just so I could say that I had bathed in the Sea of Galilee.

"You lot enjoy yourselves and I'll guard and watch over you like mother duck," I told them. A quick rub with a towel and I had my boots, khaki drill shorts and shirt on before the last one in hit the water.

After smoking a couple of cigarettes I decided to stretch my legs. Keeping within sight and earshot of my mates I walked alongside the gently lapping sea, turned and completed a wide half circle. By now I was feeling far from well. "Too much sun," I told myself as I came back by the water's edge. Thankfully I reached the welcome shade of the 3-tonner where 'Hursty' was having a catnap.

"You look rough Trev, here, get some liquid down you" he said offering me a drink. I gulped down the brackish contents of his water bottle. "I'll keep watch, you lie down and have a kip," he ordered.

Sleep came easier than I expected. Dreams I've had plenty of but never one so vivid, so real, so memorable as my experience at Galilee. With me in this paradise with its restful waters and tropical vegetation was the dark-haired beauty I had seen on my arrival here. She had been sipping orange juice at a roadside stall. I'd smiled at this sun-tanned girl dressed in faded blue shorts and skimpy top and to my amazement she had smiled back. Now she stood beckoning me forward. Eagerly I moved towards where she waited in the sweet scented seclusion of nearby trees.

"Go no further, it's a trap," came a voice. As if by an invisible wall my approach was halted, try as I might I couldn't move forward.

"This way," commanded the voice. My footsteps took me to where I could see two men and the dark haired beauty leaving the cover of the trees in a hurry.

"Put down your gun and sit with me," said the voice.

"Who are you?" I asked

"I am the one who has saved you," came the reply.

I sat down with my rifle by my side. I sensed a presence but saw nothing.

"Here at this place where you sit a teacher spoke to the people of God's love and said unto them, 'Love one another and there will be no more wars, the strong will aid the weak, the rich and powerful will end the poverty and famine of their creation, the few will not oppress the many, the many will not pillage the few. This is the way to the Kingdom of Heaven.' He spoke simply so that all could understand. Since that time his words have been manipulated and his teachings distorted to comply with the desires of man and his institutions; to express compassion for the weak while adulating that which saps their strength, and to pity the starving while justifying the greed that causes their famine. Tell your people what I have told you!" "I will," I promised.

I woke up feeling refreshed and no longer feverish. All the lads were out of the water drying themselves and getting dressed. "Never felt better," I replied in answer to their queries.

We left just after 3 pm. Having missed tiffin at 1 pm, we were all looking forward to the highlight of the day, dinner in a couple of hours time. At the place where I had first seen the dark-haired girl there was no sign of the roadside stall; it was as if it had never existed. For a moment or two I thought of asking Frank Tranter and Gordon Horridge at the side of me in the cab, if they had noticed the stall on the way in, but I decided to keep quiet.

That night I lay awake on my bed long after 'Lights Out,' turning the events of the day over and over in my mind. The wayside stall could easily have packed up and gone. While it was strange for any Jew, let alone a young and attractive female to show any sign of friendship to a British soldier, the girl and her two associates seemed real enough, as did the possibility of a trap. It was the voice and the invisible presence I found hard to come to terms with. Maybe it was a figment of my imagination, yet it seemed so real. Real, like my hallucinations appeared to be when I was rushed to the Field Hospital in Greece with fever. It could be that another bout was upon me, yet I have no symptoms. Perhaps I've been out in the sun too long. By the flickering light of a candle I wrote down what I had been told on the shore of the Sea of Galilee.

Chapter 2

Illegal Immigrants

We received the welcome we had come to expect from the Jews. Some of our comrades had quite a struggle boarding the *San Dimitrio*. All of us were left in no doubts about our unpopularity.

Made secure in Haifa harbour, with a tug preventing her from capsizing, the 75-year-old, 750-ton vessel listed dangerously to port. She had taken some twelve days to cross the Mediterranean. Hanging on to the rail on the starboard side, I looked down the steeply sloping deck of this most unseaworthy ship and I was convinced that a guardian angel had sailed with the *San Dimitrio*.

All of us were aware of the ever-growing numbers of illegal immigrants trying to enter Palestine and this was the largest single attempt yet.

Our orders are to transfer the passengers to two British ships and take them to Cyprus. "Minimum force to be used at all times and no retaliation, whatever the provocation."

The stench of unwashed bodies and the unsanitary conditions of this vastly overcrowded ship assail my nostrils. These fellow human beings with the deathly pallor of the ghetto and concentration camp on their skin, with all their belongings in rag-bag bundles, under arms and strung round necks and over shoulders. Every face is etched with the mark of suffering. We stand between them and their 'promised land,' their hopes and desires. So great is my pity I want to stand aside and say to them "You have suffered enough, go and make your new homes and good luck to you."

Some have the bowed heads and downcast eyes of those whose hopes have been cruelly dashed. Others have staring, frightened eyes, reflecting hurt and misery. For a brief moment my piece of chocolate brought a spark of happiness, to be replaced by even more misery when a man's hand snatched the chocolate and threw it down at my feet. He spat out words which were foreign to me but their meaning was clear.

"Calling you names won't hurt you," they told me when I was a young boy; well, they were wrong. These Jews with eyes that blaze hate at me and call me 'Nazi bastard' and 'fascist swine' are hurting me. So are their sly kicks to my shins and I feel defiled by their spittle on my skin and my clothing.

My pity is replaced by a burning hate of these people. Have they forgotten so soon that it was Britain that stood alone against their Nazi persecutors while other countries dithered? Up until recently Briton and Jew stood shoulder to shoulder in a common cause; now, by the politicians, we are divided.

Some in our ranks fought in North Africa and Italy. How do they feel, I wonder? I look across at Lofty Rendle; he joined up under age and went through the hell of Arnhem with a battery of Light Air. Too many painful memories for him to talk about, but he is always willing to express his appreciation of the valiant Dutch who sheltered and helped him and others, during Operation 'Market Garden.' His hate for these Jews who spit in his face and call him a Nazi bastard must be more intense than my own.

"Hold steady, lads!" comes the word of command from the Sergeant-Major. Despite all the insults and provocation, our discipline prevents any retaliation and well they knew it and they take advantage of it. I look left and right along the line of my fellow gunners who wear the white spearhead of the 1st Infantry Division and I am proud to be in such company and glad that we are able to 'turn the other cheek.'

White de-lousing powder showing up on their dark clothing, they shuffle off the *San Dimitrio*. Half covered with oilskin and bound with a frayed leather belt the bundle dropped near my feet. Instinctively I bent down, picked it up and handed it back to a lady dressed all in black. She smiled her thanks and gently touched my hand. Thin and unkempt, her dark clothing emphasised the waxen pallor of her finely chiselled face. Her smile showed even white teeth and lit up her big brown eyes under which were rings as black as her shoulder length raven hair. A few good dinners, a fortnight in the sun, bathed and groomed and dressed in some new attire and here is a young lady with such beauty as to rival Hollywood's best. If anyone should ask, "What value is a flicker of friendship from just one among the so many that hate you?," my reply would be, "Of a value sufficient to make me forget my hate for a while and sufficient for me to know that I shall remember her smile and her touch to the end of my days."

Down the ramp and along the dockside, fellow gunners had put aside their steel helmets for berets and some of the weak and overburdened had put aside their hate and were allowing the soldiers to give them a helping hand.

I watched the lady in black walk slowly to the Cyprus-bound ship. She turned, looked back, smiled and gave a brief wave. I waved back, "Love one another," I murmured to myself.

This time I heard no voice but I felt the presence I had first encountered at Galilee. Conspicuous amongst the khaki drill of soldiers and the drab dress of immigrants was a figure in a none too white robe with a hand raised as though in recognition. Before I could wave back the figure was gone. Unless it was a figment of my imagination I had just experienced another visit of the Galilean.

Illegal immigrants totalling 1,279 were successfully taken off the

San Dimitrio and put aboard the *Empire Heywood* and the *Ocean Vigour*. The worst part of our task was over.

Alert and on guard I looked down through the hatch at the passengers below. Some slept the sleep of exhaustion, others blazed with a hate that denied them sleep. Loud cursing further along the deck brought smiles to our faces. A voice of authority rings out and all is quiet again. "What was that all about?" I enquired of 'Knocker' Hall when he came to relieve me.

"Paddy's been down with a bucket of tea for the Jews and one of the bastards tripped him up and he's scalded his bloody foot!"

With our charges safely delivered to Cyprus, gone is the provocation that sorely tested my willpower; gone is the malevolence that seemed to intrude on my very soul.

With my eyes closed I try to think of the nice things in life, of loved ones and home, but it is those we are leaving behind in the internment camps that command my thoughts. Without doubt, they have suffered long and harshly under the yoke of oppression; many will have known nothing else. Theirs has been a world where 'might is right and merciless' and many who have known no mercy (as we know to our cost) show no mercy. They see our acceptance of their insults and our refusal to retaliate as weakness.

The Royal Navy will continue to intercept the larger and most of the other illegal-immigrant ships. We shall continue to tranship the passengers and take them to Cyprus. Many are the ways of entering Palestine in ones and twos and in groups they arrive under cover of darkness. Their numbers grow with each day that passes and so do our troubles. Oh! If we could keep on sailing, the air is clean and fresh. We can relax without courting danger, and enjoy the shimmering beauty of the sea and the ever-changing skies. In this little world there is peace, perfect peace, and it's ours to bask in until we dock at Haifa later today, November 2nd 1946.

Chapter 3

Guard Duty

In the belief that life couldn't be much worse I decide to break the soldier's golden rule and volunteer for almost anything.

Guard duties take up most of my life. Two hours on and four hours off throughout the night and it comes round with monotonous regularity. Prior to guard-mounting parade, I clean and check my rifle and that makes sense to me. What follows does not! Webbing equipment has to be scrubbed and bleached white and sometimes even made whiter with Blanco, which makes me more visible! The noise made by my metal-studded boots sounds good on the parade ground but announces my comings and goings. Brasses and leather 'bulled up' like mirrors reflect the light. All very nice at Buckingham Palace but this is Palestine! In the Army, orders are obeyed, not questioned, as I found to my cost some months ago. We scrub and polish trying to outshine each other for the reward of being selected as 'stick man.'

After inspection, orders are read out. "Keep alert at all times. Follow the correct procedure for challenging anyone who approaches. *Do not* fire unless fired upon. Under *no* circumstances do you fire on women and children."

"Halt, who goes there?"

"Orderly officer!"

"Advance and be recognised!"

"All quiet?" he asked, looking relieved when I shouldered the rifle that had been pointing at his chest.

"Yes sir"

"Nothing to report?"

"No sir."

"Good man. Carry on, gunner."

From past experience I know that my spirit is at its lowest ebb between midnight and 4 am. Unwelcome is the moon that bathes me and my beat in its light. Meshed fence and broad belt of barbed wire reflect a dull metallic gleam. On the other side the moonlight plays among the topmost branches of the dense grove, but does not penetrate the dark depths beneath. In there, less than thirty yards away, could be danger, a danger that fingers and racks every nerve in my body. Just after half-past two the whole world seems asleep, but up and down this 'Holy Land' many hundreds like me are on sentry-go. Vulnerable in the moonlight, hamstrung by orders and procedures, all of us know that both the 1st Div and the 6th Airborne Div are taking casualties. Who among us will lose his life to the terrorist bullet or bomb before cockcrow?

My ears strain for a tell-tale sound; my eyes are unblinking. At the flutter of a moth my arsehole tightens to the size of a shirt button. I hold my breath, let it out and take air in again silently, I think of our numbers, I think of our casualties, the odds should be long enough to give me comfort but they don't, and every stride I take my boots crunch.

"Down!" the voice and the thrust came together, as I went sideways and down, the whip crack of a bullet passed my left ear. Hitting the ground I instinctively fired in the direction of the flash I had seen in the darkness of the grove. Rifles and Bren guns opened fire, the guard turned out, the camp was awake.

"Cease firing!" came the shouted command. "Who fired first?" If I said "Me, sir" the next question would be "Why?" My reply would have to be "Because I was fired at but wasn't hit, thanks to the Galilean (who seemingly only I can hear) shouting a warning and pushing me out of harm's way."

"Who fired first?" the orderly officer asked again and once more his question went unanswered. It was made clear to all of us that any more indiscriminate firing would incur severe punishment.

The events relieved the monotony and provided a talking point for all.

"Sure, there's nothing eases the tension like the kick of a rifle in the shoulder," and few would disagree with Paddy about that.

With every day that passes, Palestine Arabs grow more resentful of the Jews who continue to multiply and spread. "Unfair," cry the Arabs, "The oppressed are becoming the oppressors and you stand by and protect them!" "Unfair," cry the Jews "You intern and imprison our people and deny us our homeland!"

"Yes, I do all of these things. My actions stretch my friendship with you Arabs to breaking point. At the same time I stoke up the murderous hate you Jews have for me. Yet, I am but a 19-year-old gunner, conscripted to fight in World War 2. Before that, I was a bread van driver for the Co-op, in a world where my biggest problem was trying to share out a wartime quota of four dozen small fancy cakes between twelve dozen clamouring housewives!"

Less than three weeks to Christmas. Will the Jewish terrorists mark the event with an atrocity like the one of last July? On the 22nd of that month they blew up British HQ Palestine in Jerusalem's King David Hotel. The resultant death toll of 91, including civilians and passers-by, focussed the world's attention on Palestine.

Countries expressed their condemnation pf those who perpetrated the atrocity, but countries, like people, can have two faces, and the terrorist in the eyes of one, is a freedom fighter in the eyes of the other!

Ever-present danger commands my awareness, yet there are long periods when time hangs heavy. A letter from home is read over and over again. My five cigarettes a day have jumped to fifteen a day. I draw deep into my lungs every wisp of smoke and hold it till it is spent.

Every meal, every sit-down visit to the latrine are highlights of the day. Taking a quick bite out of a lump of bread to see how many lightning-fast weevils I can spot before they disappear again, is amusing but not to everyone's taste. 'Phantom' with his poker face is unrivalled at bringing us light relief but sometimes it exacts a heavy price on others. On parades, especially the more important ones I try without success to keep well away from 'Phantom.' He follows me and forms up by my side. "Come what may we have to stick together!" he says with a grin. Webbing gleaming white with blanco, brasses shining. "Parade, Shun!" Highly polished boots rise, fall and thud the sand as one. Chest out, stomach in, thumbs down seams of K.D. shorts.

Always on every parade there are long spells of complete silence as if everyone has turned to stone, and these are the periods when 'Phantom' does his 'party trick'! He varies his time, so only he knows when it is going to happen. It could be now. "Open order, march!" or while they walk up and down our ranks. "Please don't let it happen while the officer is inspecting me or looking down my rifle barrel." He and his aides moved on. I gave a gentle sigh of relief. The Sergeant-Major frowned at me for breathing out loud. It came just as I was beginning to relax. Never noticeably forced, always one, two, three, drill timing seconds in duration. Sonorous, shameless fart, loitering lazy and heavy, with no breeze and no movement to shift it. The high ranking and well bred officer noisily clears his throat and looks skywards, but nothing stirs up there. His white knees betraying his recent arrival from the UK the young Second Lieutenant's face reddens as though he is the guilty one. In a face burnt the colour of mahogany, the unblinking eyes of the Sergeant-Major glare in my direction. 'Phantom,' I know full well, won't be moving a muscle. I bite my tongue until it bleeds; the tense silence is almost unbearable. I am at breaking point when away to the left of me, some poor sod tittered, then another and another. "Silence in the ranks!" roared the Sergeant-Major. "Take their names, Bombardier!"

In the short space of time before silence returned, I took a few deep breaths and regained control of myself. I think of 'Phantom' and I think of vengeance, but as always that will evaporate and be replaced with laughter when the parade is over.

Life goes on, nightly curfews continue. Guard duties are increased, patrols are stepped up. The 'Stern Gang' and the 'Irgun Zvai Leumi' with their mines, bombs and bullets, cause ever increasing bloodshed and most of the blood is British.

Chapter 4

A Spell in England

They didn't believe me when I told them. "All right, go and look for yourselves, it's there on the notice board," I said with a satisfied smirk on my face.

The notice ran :

H.Q. 1st Field Regiment R.A.
Middle East Land Forces,
Ref. G/4/6.
To; O.C. 11 Bty.
O.C. 52 Bty.
O.C. RHQ. Troop. 19th December 1946

The following O.Rs are nominated to attend the following courses at BORDON, HANTS.

14090805	P/A/ Bdr. Caves R.P. (A19)	14 Jan–22 April.
14872600	Gnr. Watts J.T. (A19)	14 Jan–22 April.
14941923	Gnr. Hall T .(B17)	14 Jan–22 April.

Report to Regimental MI Room for FFI 0830 hrs. 20th Dec.1946.

Movement will take place 0500 hrs. Saturday 21 Dec 46 to Haifa Central Station for onward transmission to 156 Transit Camp, Port Said and onward routing to the UK

"You jammy bugger," was the only printable comment among the many made on their return.

"How the hell have you wangled that?"

"You're some bugger's blue eyed boy, that's for sure!"

I waited for them to quieten down before I spoke.

"Do as I do, when they ask for volunteers put your hands up!"

"Not on your bloody Nelly!"

"You'll drop a bollock one of these days, Lofty!"

"Until then, my friends," I said with a grin, "I shall make the best of my good fortune."

The train journey from Haifa to Gaza proved uneventful. A little further on at Rafah on the border with Egypt, a figure dressed in a white robe raised a hand in farewell and was gone before I could wave back. I knew it was the Galilean.

On Christmas Eve I handed in my rifle and 50 rounds of ammunition to the QM at Port Said Transit Camp before embarking on the first stage of the MEDLOC Route to the UK. After the heat of the Middle East I was looking forward to the more moderate temperature of Southern France.

Hyères so beautiful, yet the palm trees, tropical shrubs and plants look a mite sad, and no wonder, for the wind blows cold. This unusual winter is extending icy fingers into places new. Under blue skies on the Côte d'Azur I don my Army greatcoat. It seemed to get colder with every hour that passed on the long rail journey, up through France to Calais. At Dover, it just felt good to be back in Britain. Winter had Bordon in its grip throughout my time there and I never felt really warm. In the Peak District they were experiencing far worse. Tideswell had been cut off by blizzards. Numbers 1 and 2 Alma Cottages have drifted snow up to and covering the bedroom windows. Tunnels dug through the snow are the only ways in and out of the houses.

March 11th. After completing the course successfully, I am upgraded to 2 stars, awarded a pay increase, and on my way home for 30 days leave.

In the hills, things are getting back to normal. All but a few minor roads are open. In the fields, under the limestone walls and by the roadside, shrunken drifts of snow linger. Among my loved ones, in front of a roaring coal fire I feel warm again. A home-cooked meal, a night's sound sleep and no bugle blowing 'Reveille.' It is as if I have never been away.

Sweet sixteen just one week ago, Stella Kirby of Sherwood Road, Tideswell, and myself start going out together. My school-mate Harry Ball, serving with the Northamptonshire Regiment in India, is home on leave. We spend a bit of time together and have a day out in Glossop.

Never did 30 days go so quick. Spring is in the air, buds unfurling, birds singing. It is April the 10th and duty calls me back to Palestine.

Chapter 5

Palestine Again

The S.S. *Orduna* docked at Malta for a few hours before carrying on to Port Said.

"You've not kept it very clean," I remarked to the QMS as I blew some imaginary dust off my rifle. He scowled, shoved 50 rounds of ammo towards me and grunted, "Sign here and here!"

I wasn't going back to the 1st Field Regiment at Ramat David. The 1st Infantry Division and the 6th Airborne Division had swapped places in my absence. Camp 21 at Kfar Yona near Nathanya was my destination. Off the train and on to the waiting 3-tonner. Among the escorts I saw the familiar face of John Mills. He told me that the 1st Field Regiment RA had moved to Camp 21 at the end of January and been redesignated 59th Field Regt RA on April 1st. Some of the lads, including Gerry Burr, had gone to 41st Field Regt RA and my old mob, the Bengal Rocket Troop, was with 132 Battery. I was going to 113 Battery. "That's bloody typical of the Army," I moaned. "By the looks of all the security, I gather things haven't improved."

"Got worse if anything," he replied. "A few weeks after you'd gone to Blighty the terrorists bombed the Police HQ in Haifa. I believe there were over a hundred casualties. Apart from that, it's the usual stuff. Blowing up our vehicles with mines is, like the casualties, on the increase. Our camp at Kfar Yona has been attacked with mortar and gunfire. Two other camps at Nathanya have also been attacked."

Although the journey to the Camp was short I learned much. He told me that Martial Law had been enforced and that he and most of the others had been on cordon and search (Operation 'Elephant') for 16 days at Petah Tiqvah. John's reputation for detail and accuracy is well known. I suppose that's one of the reasons they gave him a stripe to wear on his arm.

We pulled up rather abruptly at the Camp entrance. The dust cloud we brought with us enveloped and took the shine off the unfortunate gunner on guard duty. One at a time, he rubbed the toes of his boots on the back of his K.D. trousers, then with a shrug of his shoulders he let us through.

"Don't stand out in the sun too long, Shadow," I called out as we passed by. "Lofty Hall, come back to haunt us," he replied with a grin. Often in the background, 'Shadow' is attracted to dark corners and shade. If he is on a photograph and there is a shadow, then that's where he is.

This seemed to be a much bigger camp than the one at Ramat David. My spirits lifted as I walked through the Battery Lines and met up with a number of familiar faces, including the three Derbyshire lads. Roy Hurst from Derby, Roy Herod from Borrowash and Bill Wilson from Barlow. The two Roys were in my allocated tent, and like the other three occupants, were pals of mine of long standing.

"What are things like in this area?" I asked.

"Much the same," said 'Slim' Horridge, "although we did have an Army Cinema until the terrorists blew it up a couple of weeks ago."

"Any casualties?"

"Luckily only four. It could have been a hell of a lot more!"

"I'm off to the NAAFI, anybody coming?" enquired Hursty. Trant, Herod and I went off with him.

We obtained our beers and joined a bloke who was sitting on his own. I knew him only as 'Scouse.' He had served with me in Greece, at Glyfada, and at Ramat David. I didn't know his proper name, but there were dozens like that.

'Scouse' talked non-stop, mostly about Liverpool and the tough area from whence he came. On and on he droned. Our attempts to change the conversation succeeded for a short while, then it was back to Scotland Road again.

"I wonder what they're celebrating over there?" I said, looking across to the far corner where four blokes were huddled round a table full of 'Gold Star' bottles.

"I don't know, but I've got a bloody good idea," replied Scouse. Drawing his chair close to mine he said in lowered tones, "While you was away the RA Band came to play for us and a clarinet went missing. There was a right bloody flap on."

"There was a thorough search, but nothing was found!"

"How do you know?" he asked, looking puzzled.

"I don't, I'm just guessing, carry on."

"Well, you're effing right, it wasn't found, but since then, Lofty Rendle and his three mates have been drinking more ale in a night than us buggers can afford in a month."

"Perhaps one of them has come into a legacy!" I suggested.

"Legacy my arse, a pound to a pinch of shit they lifted the clarinet and sold it on. Keep what I'm telling you to yourselves," he said, looking at each of us in turn. "They're hard buggers, that lot, especially Lofty Rendle, he's always effing fighting."

"There's one sure way to find out if they lifted the clarinet," I said. Standing up I looked across at Lofty Rendle and began to play an imaginary clarinet.

"You've pissed on the chips now, he's coming and he's got a bottle in each hand!" Scouse's chair tipped over and he left half a bottle of beer behind in his haste to get out.

"What's up with him?" asked Lofty, as Scouse shot out of the door.

"He's been caught short," I replied.

"Have a drink Trev, I've not seen you for ages, I thought the bloody Jews had got you!"

"I've been back home on a course and a spot of leave for three months or so"

"Lucky sod! From your antics just now I gather you know about the mystery of the missing clarinet," he said with a twinkle in his eye.

"I've heard a bit and guessed a bit," I replied with a grin.

A couple of drinks later his mates and mine departed. We stayed behind talking.

"Do you know that while you were away, some of your mob burned a tent down?"

"No, what happened?" I asked.

"They were brewing up on that dodgy stove you brought from Egypt. It either blew up or tipped up and the whole caboodle went up in flames, including rifles and ammo. Bloody bullets flying everywhere."

"Anybody hurt?"

"No, it was a good laugh really. Let's have another drink, I'll pay," he said.

The following afternoon, having finished duties for the day, Roy Herod and I were looking through some photos Les Mace had given him while I'd been away.

"Les has done two of these, one for you and one for me," he said, passing me a photo featuring the pair of us standing either side of a notice board inscribed "Crusaders Cemetery" in Arabic and English.

"Do you remember the name of the place where this was taken?" I asked him

"Caesarea rings a bell, but I'm not sure."

"I thought it was Athlit."

"Does it matter?"

"You know, Roy, I used to ask my mother that when she wrote names and dates on the back of her photos. At the time I laughed and pulled her leg about it, but I've come to realise since that her way is the right way."

"Talking of mothers reminds me that I've a letter to post."

Within moments of Roy leaving, a visitor arrived.

"Glad to see you again, Lofty Trev" said the GSO entering the tent and shaking me by the hand. Others may give him and his job crude names, but I address him rather grandly as GSO (General Sanitary Orderly). On less formal occasions I call him 'Violets' which he finds quite amusing.

"I bet Les Mace took that, it's a pity we've lost him" he remarked looking at the photo in my hand.

"What do you mean, lost him?"

"He's gone to 48th Field at Camp 7, he served with you in Greece didn't he?" he asked all in one breath.

"We were a long way apart, actually, he was near Eleftheroupolis, try saying that without your false teeth in, Violets."

"I haven't got false teeth!"

"Anyway, he was up north in Macedonia, and I was down near Athens."

"I know," Les said "that you was a lucky bugger living it up among beautiful bints, while he was in the freezing mountains miles from anywhere."

"It was nothing to do with luck, Violets. Someone at HQ said "Mace hails from the flatlands of Suffolk, he shall be sent up into the mountains. Hall, who comes from the High Peaks of Derbyshire, shall go forth on to the plains!"

"That deserves a fag," said Violets with a laugh. He opened up a battered tin of off-white, flattish cigarettes. We lit up together and immediately the intake of acrid smoke sent me into a coughing fit.

"Where on earth did you get them from?" I gasped, stubbing out the evil smelling cig.

"I bought 'em off Abdul, they're ever so cheap!"

"So is dried camel shit!"

"They're alright when you get used to them. Anyway, to go back to Les Mace. He told me that apart from terrorists, they had wolves galore up in the Greek mountains."

"I'm not surprised, we had wolves in the Derbyshire hills."

"Pull the other one!"

"It's perfectly true, although I must admit it was a few hundred years ago!"

"I've never been to Derbyshire," Violets said wistfully. I scribbled my home address – 2, Alma Cottages, Alma Road, Tideswell, Near Buxton, Derbyshire, on a piece of paper and gave it to him.

"If we survive and get back to civvy street, and you get a week to spare, look me up at Tideswell with its 'Cathedral of the Peak.' I'll take you up Summer Cross and on through Monks Dale, across green fields to Chee Dale and Wormhill where the last wolves in England were killed in 1490. A few more miles to Buxton, famous for its waters, Gardens, Crescent and dome. Solomon's Temple high above, Poole's Cavern far below. Millers Dale, Monsal Dale and Lathkill Dale. Bakewell of pudding fame. From Haddon Hall to High Tor and the Heights of Abraham, caves and petrifying wells of the Matlocks. Chatsworth House, Curbar Gap and Froggatt Edge, Moon Hill and Black Harry. The Three Stags Heads and what's left of the old gibbet at Wardlow Mires. Eyam's Plague Cottage and high above, Mompesson's

Well and higher still the Barrel Inn. By Hucklow Edge and Bradwell Edge or Bretton Clough and Abney into the valley where Little John and Blue John both lie buried. Win Hill and Lose Hill, Ladybower and Derwent dams. Snake Pass, Kinder Scout and Edale. Over Shivering Mountain down Winnats Pass to the castle and caverns of Castleton. There I will show you the Devil's Arse. Then we will take our ease and have a drink in one or more of the nine friendly pubs in Tideswell."

"That sounds bloody lovely, Trev, roll on demob."

"Have you heard of Lord Byron?" I asked.

"Yes," said Violets, "he was a proper poet not a shithouse poet like a lot of them round here."

"Well," he wrote "there are things in Derbyshire as noble as in Greece," and he didn't see half as much as I'll show you!"

Suspects awaiting release after a search for illegal weapons, Rehovoth, 5th March 1947

Chapter 6

Home Thoughts from Abroad

Into the month of May, and as I write home to my loved ones, I think of hawthorn blossom in Monks Dale and Millers Dale, flaunting colours of red but mostly white and sometimes pink where they've crossed. I think of Tideswell Brook and 'jacksharps,' and the trout-rich Wye which it joins at Litton Mill. Kingfishers darting, new life in the water. Birdsong greeting new green in the trees.

I pass by the clattering Mill that gave this hamlet its name. Sadness brings a tear to my eye, when I think that a little over a century ago, girls and boys, 10 years old and upwards were brought here like cattle from Workhouses far away. Slaves whose home was overcrowded, dark and dank. Half starved on a diet of what can only be described as 'pigswill,' they worked 16 hours a day for six days a week. Urging them to greater efforts, the cruel Mill-owner and his five sons, armed with sticks, handed out beatings.

On Sundays most of the children cleaned the Mill and its machinery. Others whose clothes were not in rags walked under supervision to Tideswell Church. So high was the mortality among them, that, in order to lessen the public outcry the burials were divided between Tideswell and Tappington.

"Suffer the little children to come unto me!"

Now above the noise of shuttles the shouts are friendly, there is laughter, the Devil no longer holds sway.

I follow the river as it flows. I close my eyes and follow my nose. Wild garlic so pungent every step of the way. Now another smell mingles; just a whiff now and then, faint at first but getting stronger, comes the refreshing scent of aromatic peppermint. I know where I've got to, before I open my eyes to see the huge cotton mill and Monsal Dale beyond. I'm at Cressbrook.

Another day, later on, the sweet perfume of a fragrance like no other, will lead me up those wooded and alpine slopes to where the exquisite 'Lily of the Valley' grows. I think of her tiny bells of purest white and perfect form. I think of her leaves and delicate stem of flawless green. I think of her dancing and swaying to the whims of the breeze. I think of heaven, I think she's halfway there.

My letters are written; my dreams of home are over for the present. It's business as usual here in the Holy Land. Mostly continuous guard duties, two hours on, four hours off, with no let-up from the terrorists.

First week in June, two trains are derailed by mines. A railway station is bombed and on the 9th, two policemen are kidnapped. Our spirits lift over the following days when the kidnapped policemen are recovered and other attempts to kidnap and blow up the Army HQ at Tel Aviv are thwarted. Thankfully, up to now, this month's casualties seem to be lighter than usual.

The end of the month draws near. I take up my pen, I think of home. Tideswell Wakes will be in full swing. All the fun of the fair will be in Market Square. Sports and concerts, fancy dress and carnival, morris dancing, torchlight procession and 'Sunday School walk.' Much in demand, Tideswell Silver Prize Band will be answering the call, doing their duty and more.

I looked up as Knocker Hall came in to the tent; I could tell by his troubled expression that something was wrong.

"The bastards have shot seven of our lads!"

"Where at?"

"Three at Haifa and four at Tel Aviv, I don't know their names or their regiments."

I looked at my letter that I had only just started. It was dated June 28th 1947. I screwed it into a ball and put my pen away.

The following day 29th June 1947. *Location* HERZLIYIOA. Shooting attack on soldiers – three casualties. Only here in Palestine do I experience difficulty in finding something to write about. With regularity I pass through, or by, the biblical places I first learned about at home, and at Tideswell's High Street Methodist Sunday School. Every such occasion awakens great interest within me, but always, it is danger that commands my attention and draws my eyes elsewhere.

I see the orange trees and water melon plants, for often, I pick and eat their sweet and juicy fruits. Wild flowers grow in great profusion but I can describe but few. At the roadsides as I drive and in their swathes as I tread, those blooms could be hiding a mine. Birds of many species fly overhead but I rarely look up to the skies. Sweet birdsong either stays in the background or goes unheard, for my ears are cocked for more sinister sounds.

"Hard work, this letter writing," Slim's remark brought murmurs of agreement from all of us sat round the canteen table with pens and notepads.

"Come to think of it though, Yorky who joined us from the 4th Indian Division always found writing letters a doddle." I added with a grin.

"I remember him, he always had a running sore on his face, it cost me two beers for his red shite-hawk" said Scouse who had acquired quite a collection of Divisional shoulder flashes.

"Refresh our memories, Lofty," urged Roy Herod, pouring half of his bottle of 'Gold Star' into my glass.

"For those of you who don't go back that far, Yorky had, as Scouse says, a large and festering blemish on the left cheek of his face. He was one of those unfortunate sods with a dark complexion and facial hair that grew fast and strong. From time to time, Sergeant-Majors came down hard on him. "You may be on Active Service but that's no excuse for looking like a bloody tramp. You're on a charge, fall out and get a shave!"

"As soon as he was out of earshot he would give tongue, "Fuck the Sergeant-Major!" Then lathering up vigorously, "Fuck the Army!" followed by "Fuck 'em all!" Glaring at himself through his mirror and wielding a razor, with a hand made unsteady by his fervour, he would attempt the impossible. Always starting on the left side of his face he would try to shave off hair that was still below the skin. When he cried "Fuck it!" at the top of his voice, all within hearing knew that he had sliced the scab off his sore again. As you can gather, he was quite a character. All of us were fascinated by the speed with which he completed his letters. Hunched over with his nose almost touching the paper, head on one side and tongue lolling out, he would begin. A few minutes later his tongue would go back in. He'd finished while we were still thinking what we could write about.

One day, curiosity got the better of me. Offering Yorky a cigarette, I purposely let it fall from my fingers. When he bent down to pick it up I saw what he had written.

Dear Mam, Dad and Pearl,

I am alright, Hope dog is. Looking forward to coming home. I will write again soon. Hoping this finds you as it leaves me, in good health.

Your loving son, Horace.

Not wanting him to think that I had read his letter I asked "Are you writing to your girl friend, Yorky?"

"No, I'm writing to my parents. I'll be bloody glad when I'm back home with them and my dog."

"What do you call your dog?"

"Pearl," he said, with a wistful look in his eyes."

We could all learn from Yorky. He wrote home with greater frequency than any of us and he told his loved ones what was important to them. Fully aware of the fact that it is enough to witness and experience the actions perpetrated by these terrorists, without writing home about it, we rack our brains to think of something to fill a page or two.

Lofty Rendle's arrival jogged my memory of a recent event and set my pen in motion.

Away from camp down near Petah Tiqvah all was quiet. Then came the faint sound of hooves on tarmac.

"Halt, who goes there?" Judging by the southern accent it was either John Mills or Jim Wiley making the challenge just out of sight round the bend in the road.

"Brigadier Bigballs, inspecting troops of the 1st Guards Brigade!" The answer was followed by laughter.

Into our vision came Lofty astride a requisitioned donkey. He halted outside the Bren-gun pit. "Well done, top hole chaps, you're a fine body of men. When I've done my rounds I shall allow you to have rides on my noble steed at a special rate." The donkey seemed to have taken quite a shine to 'Lofty' whose commands were accompanied not by the whack of a stick but by the reward of a mint humbug.

"Walk on," he ordered.

"Come back here Gunner Rendle, at once!" came the shouted counter order from the Battery Captain. Lofty's feet which touched the ground played an effective part in helping his mount to perform a rapid turn around. At a brisk trot they headed back to the irate officer and a wailing Arab tugging at the Captain's arm demanding 'backsheesh' for the use of his ass.

My letter writing done, I finished my beer and returned to the tent to get my head down. Tomorrow I am on 12-hour guard duty again.

Chapter 7

Dog

"Anything happened during the night?" asked 'Hursty' as I joined him for breakfast.

"No, we've had a quiet night, thank God. By the way, Hursty, as I came off duty I caught a glimpse of Dog. I'm glad you brought him with you. The last time I saw him was at Ramat David before Christmas."

"We didn't bring him, he just appeared."

We had been in this camp for a couple of weeks or so when Dog was found near the main gate. He was more or less out on his feet. One of the lads picked him up and carried him into the Guardroom. They watered him, fed him and gave him a wash and handed him over to one of the medics. It took him over a week to recover. Now, apart from a limp, he's OK and back on the booze again."

Scruffy mongrel he might have been, but he had come some 40 miles and found us amongst the thousands of other soldiers. Good old Dog. He came among us, seemingly out of nowhere, when we first arrived from Greece. Without doubt there was terrier in him. But what else, is anybody's guess. Roughish haired, drab desert colour, he had a splash of white round his mouth and quite a lot of black on large ears that flop and looked out of place on him. With the best will in the world he can't be described as anything like good looking. He is nobody's pet; sometimes he allows us to stroke him, at other times he warns us off with a growl. Like us, he gets his food from the cookhouse and sleeps when and where he can. He never gets under our feet and most of the time he goes unnoticed.

When he joined us he was referred to by a goodly number of monikers, mostly 'Lad,' 'Boy,' 'Scruff,' and 'Scruffy.' All that changed when the Orderly Officer came across him near the bins behind the cookhouse.

"What have we here, Bombardier?" he asked.

"It's a dog sir!"

"Dog! Dog! I know it's a bloody dog, Bombardier!"

By this time the animal had vanished. Its official name, 'Dog! Dog! I know it's a bloody dog, Bombardier!' spread by word of mouth round the camp. Now we just call him Dog.

The day after Dog had been dubbed was pay-day and the 21st birthday of a bloke in our Troop. Also, it was the eve of departure for two lucky sods who were going home for demob. We had much to celebrate, the NAAFI was full, the Gold Star was flowing. Dog, hidden under our table, popped his head out every now and then to lap up an ashtray full of beer. With every round of drinks the ashtray was refilled.

Taffy and Jock, tenor and baritone of some repute, led the singing. 'Nellie Dean' and 'Lilli Marlene' received encores. Much laughter accompanied the repertoire of ribald Army songs. We sang 'We'll Meet Again.' It was time to go.

"Come on Dog, let's be having you." He came out from under, went sideways like a crab, hit Paddy's legs and went down in a heap. "Come here you drunken little bugger you!" he said, picking Dog up and cradling him in his arms. "I shall have to be carrying you home, you little varmint!" but his words were lost on Dog, who was snoring like a good 'un. Paddy bedded him down by his bedside. When he awoke next morning 'Dog' had gone. Several days passed before he ventured into the NAAFI again. A quick learner, he found out his capabilities for holding his beer. Now one ashtray full a night was his limit.

Chapter 8

In the Derbyshire Hills Again

July 11th. Duties completed for the day. Unless there's an emergency, my time is my own.

Nowhere to go, no one to talk to. Three of my mates were on guard, the other two are having an afternoon nap. I've nothing to read. I could write a letter or two but there's nothing of interest to write about. As I do so often in situations like this, I close my eyes and within moments, I'm in the Derbyshire hills again.

Haymaking is in full swing, Alf and Jim Gregory's one-speed shire-horse drags the clattering mowing machine round and round on its iron wheels. Grasses of many varieties, clovers red and white, brownish purple burnet, blue cranesbill. Shades of yellow, dandelions and buttercups. Shy, light blue harebells and moonpennies in big white drifts, all cut down in their prime and laid in neat straight rows.

Sweeping scythes, sometimes hacking. Bill Shenton, along with Pat Frain and his brother Tom, downing the herbage near the dry limestone walls that fence the field. Stinging nettles fall in untidy heaps. Proud thistles that once looked imperiously over the wall top, weep sap as they are kicked aside to shrivel in the sun. Butterflies of many hues fluttering, all of a tither, their eggs and caterpillars with nettles and thistles lie.

Their cover destroyed, gone are the rabbits, hare and fox. Seeds, insects, mice and voles all laid bare for the taking. First in on beating wings, sparrows lead the browns, with pink of finch and yellow-hammer adding colour. Sooty jackdaws with grey doves mingle, followed in by noisy rooks. Chattering magpie, in iridescent plumage of bold black and white and last of all, wary carrion crow.

Here and there curlews cry. Overhead the lapping wings and plaintive calls of acrobatic peewits, spiralling, tumbling. Swallows swoop and dart with skilful grace. Above the chirps and chatter, the coos, caws and cries, the skylark soars. Heaven calls its own sweet songster up, holds it for a while, then lets it down to earth again.

Keeping a lonely vigil, a Little Owl sees it all from the dead branch of ash near the gate. Most of his life, like mine is spent on watch, with one eye always open.

Chapter 9

Another IZL Atrocity

July 12th, two soldiers abducted at Nathanya. Cordon and search. Detailed for cordon duties and with not far to go we are quickly into position. Cordon with thousands of eyes and ears, watching and listening. Within its confines the search begins. Night falls, the drone of military vehicles continues. The painstaking search goes on, the cordon remains unbroken.

Under the stars, on groundsheets and blankets, rest those whose turn it is for four hours off. The pattern remains unchanged as the days go by. In this area, now under Martial Law and with troops heavy on the ground, terrorist activities appear to have ceased. Elsewhere, they've stepped up their murderous work. Daily we learn of assassinations, of bombings and attacks by guns, grenades and mortars.

On July 27th Martial Law is lifted and Operation Tiger is concluded. Still missing are the two soldiers, Sergeant Clifford Martin and Sergeant Mervyn Paice.

July 31st. The bodies of our two comrades are found bound and hooded, hanging from the trees, in an orange and eucalyptus grove near Nathanya. A hidden mine beneath the corpses is discovered and made safe. One of the bodies is booby-trapped and explodes, severely injuring an officer. With the mind-numbing news comes a feeling of revulsion. Soul-tearing fury is etched on every face. The unusual silence is broken from time to time, as pent-up anger against the Jews and everything Jewish, bursts out in a curse. Atrocities against the Security Forces are a daily fact of life. In one way or another we all feel their touch, but the inhumanity of this foul deed, presses heavy and leaves an ineradicable mark. The perpetrators of this crime, the "Irgun Zvai Leumi" and their commander, Menachem Beigin, later Prime minister of Israel, have proved yet again that their barbarism knows no limits.

With great relief I am able to rest on a proper bed with a canvas roof over my head, but sleep doesn't come readily. Recent events fill my troubled mind. Anger is uppermost and confuses my thinking. I think about the grieving families of Mervyn Paice and Clifford Martin and feel deep sorrow.

"WANTED: For murder. Menachem Beigin." I don't need to look at his picture in the papers and on posters, every detail of his bespectacled face will remain imprinted in my mind forever.

The feeble light from my torch picked out the faded gold lettering on my notepad given to me on my call-up. "With best wishes, from all at Tideswell High Street Primitive Methodist Chapel and Sunday School." I thought of Wilfred and Dorothy Furness, Mr Flint, Miss Lily Townsend, Mrs Elliot and a host of others, all kind and friendly people. I wrote: "Roll on the day when I can say goodbye to the God-forsaken land of Palestine and its godless people."

Tired out in mind and body, I went to sleep doubting the very existence of God. Sometime during the hours of darkness I felt a presence. I heard the voice of someone, whose long absence had caused me to believe that he had just been a figment of my imagination.

"God has forsaken neither this land nor its people, but there are some in this land who have forsaken God!"

The Galilean had been and gone. My anger against the terrorists is undiminished but now I realised that such anger against all their race is unfair and unjust. Reaching for my diary I struck out what I had written.

Chapter 10

My Bomb

August brought a snap inspection of our kit which revealed nothing of interest to the rummaging sergeant and the watching officer.

"What do you reckon that was all about?" asked 'Slim'. Nobody seemed to know, so we came to the obvious conclusion that something had gone missing.

"You'll never guess what they found in Lofty Rendle's kit," said Taffy. "What?" asked half a dozen eager voices.

"Two French bayonets and a Mk5 bayonet with the flashring sawn off. A signal lamp and a Sten gun with the butt sawn off and two full mags of ammo. His mates said if they had known about it they would have thought twice about sharing a tent with a bloody madman." There was no mention of the grenade that I knew Lofty kept inside his best pair of boots, so I assumed that it hadn't been found. A long time ago he had told me of his resolve that after what happened at Arnhem, never again would he lack equipment and ammo in times of danger. While I can't think of anyone I'd rather have watching my back than Lofty Rendle, I did have some sympathy for his tent companions, for unlike them, I knew about the grenade in their midst, I also knew he kept it primed!

Talking of which reminds me that I've got a nine-pound bomb back home in Tideswell. I was still a schoolboy in 1940 when, on the day after the Luftwaffe blitzed Sheffield, I found this bomb amongst the debris of Fox Street in the Pitsmoor area of the city. In perfect condition with no marks or dents in it couldn't have been dropped from an aeroplane. More than likely it belonged on someone's mantelpiece.

My unique souvenir made me the envy of all my mates. I could have traded it for many things including a Hercules cycle in good condition (apart from brakes), but I already had a bike and the one Doug Summer was offering me wasn't his own. Charlie Ford's offer of an air pistol proved very tempting but in the end I decided not to exchange. For a while I stored the bomb in the old dry lavatory at the top of our garden. Eventually I brought it indoors and was ordered to take it out immediately. To prove that it wasn't dangerous I unscrewed the brass-nosed base away from the tail as I had done many times before, but it made no difference, the bomb had to go.

Like myself, all the lads and quite a few of the girls knew every shed and outbuilding that offered easy access and shelter from the weather and prying eyes. With no lock on the door, our old lavatory wasn't a safe place to keep my treasured possession in. We had no cellar at Number 2 Alma Cottage, but Uncle Colin and Aunt Sarah's cellar next door was large enough to provide dry, frost-free storage for both families; down creaking steps of wood, worn with use, blanched white with scrubbing. I never went down them without jumping with both feet together on one of the steps. It always brought the same rapid response from Aunt Sarah up above. "What do you think you're doing?"

"Trying to drive out the woodlice."

"There's no 'wick' things in my cellar, I've told you before. Now behave yourself or I'll tell your Dad!"

Cellar walls, ceiling and shelves thick with clean-smelling limewash and white as driven snow. On the top shelf, a box of assorted wicks, a dozen boxes of matches, six dozen candles and two score of empty 1-lb jam jars. Below in dark glistening rows a shelf full of home-made rhubarb and ginger jam, and round the corner a shelf of damson jam. On the cold gritstone benches, bottles of ruby red damson wine, drawn up in straight lines, fronted with a dozen jars of bright lemon curd. In the gloom at the rear, two great puncheons with nothing in and four big stone jars full of eggs, preserved in lime. Idle stands another stone jar, fitted with a wooden paddle by Uncle Colin's brother, Giles Chapman, to make a butter churn. On the flagstoned floor in 1 cwt sacks resting on boards, half a ton of Great Hucklow-grown King Edward potatoes and three sacks of swede turnips from Tideslow Farm. In the corner on a ledge away from it all, large blocks of washing soap, CWS green and red carbolic. Hanging from hooks on either side two hurricane lamps–Markovitz's best. Beneath, on boards, a pile of empty corn sacks washed and ready for use as backing for pegged rugs, makeshift aprons, capes, draught excluders or cut up to make hopples to stop sheep from jumping walls.

Into the middle of the neatly folded sacks I hid my bomb. There was a risk that it would be found in the spring when my mother and Aunt Sarah cleaned and whitewashed the cellar, but I would meet that problem when and if it arose.

Aunt Sarah came before Spring, "Your Uncle Colin has just been down the cellar to get a sack to bluff a broken hencote window up and your bomb rolled out and dropped on his foot. His nail has gone black and his big toe is the size of two. I wouldn't be a bit surprised if he didn't lose it."

"His big toe?"

"No, his nail. Don't ever put that bomb among the sacks again!"

"No, I won't, I'm very sorry. I'll put it in the far corner."

"No you mustn't. If you have to keep it in our cellar, put it out of harm's way in the cubby-hole where I keep the bucket of slaked lime."

As far as I knew it was still there. When I get back home I must do something about it.

Chapter 11

Throwing the Hammer

"The First Infantry Division, Royal Artillery sports are to be held on the 14th of August. Are there any among you who can throw the hammer?"

I came to attention and said "Yes sir."

"Well done, Hall, fall out and report to Sergeant Robson."

"How much experience have you?" asked the Sergeant, handing me a heavy metal ball with its length of wire handle.

"Not a lot and its' some while ago," I replied.

I didn't tell him that I was 10 years old, when after seeing a hammer-throwing Scot at Tideswell Picture House, I had thrown my Uncle Colin's cobbling hammer and it had gone over Mrs. Flint's garden wall, never to be recovered. The sergeant looked a bit down in the mouth so I sought to reassure him. "I'm not short of strength, when I was a schoolboy I worked for a farmer and a furniture remover. At 15 years old I worked on a coal lorry bagging and carrying." Heartened, he smiled and said "Go and practice, I'll be along later."

"Sorry sergeant, I've got to get ready for guard duties, unless you could get me off?"

"I can't do that," he said, shaking his head.

"Perhaps you could ask Captain King?"

"No!"

Never mind, I thought, it was worth a try.

There was still time for 10 minutes practice. Although it didn't go in the direction intended, my first throw gave me a great deal of satisfaction. My second attempt went higher and farther and fetched an overhead wire down near the tent lines. In biblical times they would have said something like "Begone, oh tall one, pick up thy heavy ball and get unto the wilderness forthwith!" But this is Palestine 1947, and in the tents they shout, "Piss off Lofty, yer daft sod, before yer kill some bugger!"

Obediently but not disheartened, I moved on to the next open space. Legs apart, flex my muscles, swing the hammer low and slow, higher, faster, spin around, so difficult on sand. Rhythm lost, balance gone, let go! With a crash like thunder the whirling hammer bounced off the nearby lavatory's tin roof. Shouts of alarm came from inside the doorless but not odourless circular construction. With alacrity I recovered the hammer but before I could disappear a wide-eyed Jock Ness came out from within. "What the fuck is going off?"

"It was an accident, Jock"

"I nearly shit myself, I thought it was a fucking bomb" he said, dusting some flakes of dried whitewash from his head and shoulders. He grinned, winked, turned and shouted to the lads inside "It's only Lofty Hall practising his hammer throwing. Half a dozen more throws and he'll be gone."

"Tell him to fuck off now!"

Their shouted demands were easy to comply with but not with the hammer in the place they suggested. It was time to go and get my kit bulled up for guard-mounting.

No more hammer-throwing practice, too many duties, no time, no facilities.

Tel-Litwinsky Sports Ground 10.00 hours 14th of August, not a cloud in the sky and already scorching hot. We are brought to attention and informed by the Announcer, Captain Mott, that Brigadier K F McK Lewis DSO MC RA has kindly consented to present the Divisional Artillery Athletics Challenge Shield and Individual prizes. He then read out the long list of officials starting with the President, Lt-Col Cobbold RA and ending with the Chief Marshal, Regimental Sergeant-Major Woodrow, thus ensuring that all decisions reached would go undisputed.

The Band of the 1st Bn The Suffolk Regt began to play as we lined up for our colours. HQRA–White, 20 Anti-Tank Regt.–Black, 88 LAA Regt, RA–Yellow, 41 Field Regt RA–Red, 48 Field Regt RA–Blue. We of 59 Field Regt RA were wearing the Green.

At 10.30 hours on the dot the Sports commenced. In teams of two with three throws each, Sgt Robson and myself finished up in second place. Although it was my throw that had pulled our aggregate down he shook my hand and said, "Well done, Hall." Available are Minerals, Beer, Tea and Sandwiches, all on sale, none for free. Open all day, the Officers' Bar is doing a roaring trade, so is the Bar for the Senior NCOs. Our watering hole, the Other Ranks Bar, is almost empty which is to be expected, considering the pittance we get from the Army.

Finding a seat I closed my eyes and thought of home and Sports Day on the exposed high ground of the Cliffe. Often there I sought the shelter of a dry limestone wall from squally showers and a biting wind. Underfoot the green and honest land I've known since birth.

Here from the burning sun, I seek the perfumed shade of orange and eucalyptus trees and in this tragic and dangerous land I tread with caution the ancient dust and shifting sand.

Noise aplenty on the Cliffe, laughter, arguments in abundance. Rare was the event that ran on time, or without dispute. At Tel-Litwinsky we have applause and a little merriment. No arguments, no disputes. Everything, every event on the dot running like clockwork. It is only the music that links this place with home, for when on form Tideswell Band are every bit as good as these Suffolks.

Chapter 12

Business as Usual

A September day goes by and then another without the spilling of British blood, but my hopes do not rise, for I know from experience that the morrow will dash them.

As expected, terrorist attacks resume, illegal Jewish immigrants continue to arrive, it's business as usual. A business in which I find enough backbone to accept casualties as a fact of life but not enough to stop me from jumping at my own shadow.

I thank God for the comfort I derive from the Galilean.

At the end of the month the Jews blew up Haifa police station, causing over 60 casualties. A new month comes in with the news of the arrival of more illegal Jewish immigrant ships, under RN escort. There can be little doubt that other such ships of lesser size are getting through undetected. Jews like their communes and their crops are getting ever thicker on the ground. They grow stronger nurtured by outside aid and support and the terrorist gangs they harbour among them flourish.

Rumours abound. We hear of coming changes. We also hear, that up in Haifa some Airborne lads have been wounded by mines in one of our own minefields.

October 12th, and the changes come about. In less than a year I've said goodbye to the 1st and hello to the 59th. Now it's goodbye to the 59th and hello to the 6th Field Regt RA, 'O' Battery Rocket Troop.

The ice-cold bottles of 'Gold Star' seemed to be adding heat to the argument about the changes. There was silence when Phantom studiously declared – "They reorganise things on purpose to relieve our boredom, by giving us something different to think about." Hare-brained theory or not, it went undisputed. Falling foul of him, like getting down wind of him, is not advisable.

"Pull up a chair, Trev and settle this argument." As it was on the opposite side of the table from Phantom I accepted Slim's invitation. "Tell Geordie what Troop we were in when we were with 1st Field."

"The Bengal Rocket Troop I've a badge somewhere, showing a rampant Bengal Tiger astride a red tipped rocket. The very sight of it used to send the Greek girls into raptures." "And this one in the 6th is just The Rocket Troop with colours of blue and yellow embossed LEIPZIG 1813," added Slim.

"Alright," grunted Geordie, "but I don't believe what Lofty says about that badge of his."

"I've seen it!" said 'Jock.' "He makes things up and you see things that aren't there," snorted 'Geordie.'

"And you are as thick as pig shit!" retorted 'Jock.'

This triggered off an exchange of obscenities between them. Their hackles were up, they were on their feet and almost at it. Some were egging them on, others were trying to calm them down.

Tension suddenly eased with the realisation that Phantom had departed, but not without leaving his calling card. A lot of frantic wafting dispersed the worst of it, and as its tranquillising effects wore off, the two would-be combatants began to square up again.

Paddy, who when in drink was either belligerent or sentimental, was in the latter mood. With a sad face he began to sing 'Danny Boy.' Arguments forgotten, we all sang along with him, whistling the high notes we couldn't quite reach. A night of song followed, ending with Jock and Geordie leading the singing of 'Fuck 'em all' sung to the tune of 'Bless 'em all'.

Re-organisation was still on my mind when I climbed into bed. Quietly I recited to myself what Caius Petronius had to say about reorganisation in AD 66.

"We trained hard, but it seemed that every time we were beginning to form up into teams, we would be reorganised. I was to learn later in life that we tend to meet any new situation by re-organising, and a wonderful method it can be for creating the illusion of progress, while producing inefficiency and demoralisation."

Up to now reorganisation has made us neither inefficient nor demoralised. We moan about it, but moaning is part of a soldier's life.

Overall, October is proving to be a depressing time with little to lift our spirits. The month draws to a sad end with news of a road accident involving our Airborne comrades with over a dozen losing their lives and several others injured.

Chapter 13

Secret Mission

"Where are we going to, Lofty?" asked my two escorts.

"Joining up with the Arab Legion in Transjordan," I replied with a grin. They didn't believe me so I showed them the hand-drawn route card headed "Camp 21 to Zerka, Transjordan. NB Zerka may be spelt Zarqa or in other ways."

"What are we going up there for?"

"I can't tell you, it's a top secret mission!"

"Bollocks!"

Hooked up behind the Austin 3-tonner was a large caravan camouflaged the colour of desert sand "We shall attract the attention of every bloody terrorist in the sodding land," moaned Geordie. "They aren't daft, they know only the likes of bloody generals have caravans," he continued.

"All you have to do is keep shouting out of the window 'We're only bloody gunners'," I told him.

Three miles on we came to Nathanya crossroads and turned left for Lydda, Ramleh and Latrun. Near the Bren-gun post, a young private threw up a smart salute at the sight of the caravan. Geordie and Scouse laughed, shouted "Well done that man" and saluted him back. I slowed down near the stationary armoured car of the Palestine Police. "Do you know Graham Moulson from Cressbrook?" I shouted. Looking puzzled he shook his head.

"Is this Graham Moulson in the Palestine Police?" asked Geordie.

"I think so, but I'm not certain."

"There's a hell of a lot in the Palestine Police. How do you expect to find him when you're not even sure he's here?"

"Because this is a land where strange things happen."

"Yes, and its' a land with some strange buggers in it, and you're one of them!" Scouse nodded his head in agreement.

"Keep your eyes peeled for trouble lads and let me concentrate on my driving." Mile after mile we travelled with no stops and no respite from the incessant whine of the gearbox.

"Guide me through Jerusalem, Geordie," I said, passing him the route card.

"Left off the Jaffa Road," he called out "Mea Shearim Street, Moshe Street, New Road and keep on past the Old City." We. or rather the caravan, attracted a lot of curious looks and it was a relief when we finally cleared the city and took the Jericho road.

"According to the route card it's 25 miles to Jericho and another 10 to the frontier," said Geordie.

"So what?" grunted Scouse.

"Bollocks," replied the gunner from Newcastle.

The sun was scorching and the heat in the cab was almost unbearable.

"It's a lovely day for a chauffeur-driven trip out!" I remarked with a smile.

"Lovely day my arse!" replied Scouse.

"We should have done a hundred miles by now, Lofty," said my guide, studying the route card as we approached the Allenby Bridge.

"Ninety-nine and nine tenths to be exact," I told him.

"Yes, but we aren't on the bloody bridge yet, clever bugger."

Half immersed in the River Jordan below, a white-robed figure looked up and raised a hand in greeting. I waved back.

"What are you waving at?" asked Scouse.

"Him down there in the river," I replied.

"There's nothing there, you're seeing things, you've been out in the bloody sun too long. Either that or he's trying to work his ticket," added Geordie.

Whatever the truth of the matter, of one thing I am certain; since my first meeting with the 'Galilean' I have had a reassuring feeling that in times of danger he will protect me.

The Transjordan Frontier Force greeted us with smiles of welcome. "British soldiers very good friends," said their spokesman, puffing happily on one of my 'State Express.' Four more cigarettes brought forth similar praise from his companions. It felt nice to be in a country where people were friendly and we could relax.

"Fifteen miles to Salt and straight on for another 20 miles to Amman," announced the map reader.

Climbing up the none too wide road I noticed in the rear mirror three large black limousines coming up fast. I slowed, changed down into bottom gear, pulled well into the side and waved them on. A blast of thanks from the horn of the first car full of men who looked like bodyguards. In the next limousine a bearded distinguished figure in rich Arab robes glanced up at us and gave a brief smile as they swept past.

"That was King Abdullah and he smiled at us," shouted the excited Liverpudlian.

"Bollocks!" said Geordie, whose position on the far side of the cab limited his vision.

"Scouse is right, didn't you see the Royal Standard?"

"All I saw was the arse end of three cars and a cloud of dust!" replied Geordie, sounding somewhat aggrieved.

At Amman the route card ran out. The instructions read as follows – "Zerka is another 15 miles approx: No information available, ask your way at Amman."

"Do you speak Arabic, Lofty?"

"Oh yes, and Latin and French and Greek."

"Fluently?"

"Well, I can count up to ten and say how are you, darling, very fluently!"

"Silly sod!" they chorused.

Jumping out of the lorry I said "Leave it with me, lads" and crossed the road to where a toothless old man sat in the shade. I put a cigarette in his mouth and one behind his ear. All smiles he pointed out the way to Zarqa.

"Bloody good English cigarette," he said shaking me by the hand. "Here you are my friend," I said, giving him two more cigarettes. He didn't want me to go and came back to the lorry with me babbling away in Arabic. I kept on nodding and laughing as though I knew what he was talking about. "Allah Akbar!" I shouted and set the lorry in motion. Smiling and waving he shouted back in Arabic. Among his torrent of words the only ones I could understand were 'God is Great.'

"What did he tell you?" they asked, eyeing me with newfound respect at my apparent ability to converse in Arabic.

"He told me the way to Zarqa."

"What else?"

"Well, he said that I was very handsome and he would fit me up with one of his beautiful daughters. I thanked him and said I was greatly honoured. Then I asked, what about my two mates? And he said he didn't know anyone who would fancy such a pair of ugly buggers!"

They uttered obscenities and laughed.

At Zarqa a sergeant in the Arab Legion led the way in his jeep to a tented camp in the desert. After unhooking the caravan we were provided with a meal and allotted a tent. "What's the drill, Lofty?"

"We await orders," I replied. "Meanwhile we'll eat, sleep and keep our heads down; with a bit of luck they'll forget us."

Fortunately, I was under canvas when for the first time in my life I experienced a sandstorm. It was hot instead of cold, sand instead of snow, visibility was nil and its fury was every bit as intimidating as winter blizzards in the Peak District. Time passed slowly, we were lulled into believing we really had been forgotten. It was wishful thinking; as the person in charge I was summoned to a large tent which served as HQ.

"You should have been back with your unit by now," said the British officer.

"We have been awaiting movement orders, sir."

"Well now you have them," he barked. "Move out 0800 hours

tomorrow."

"Very good, sir."

Next morning, minus the caravan, we set off on the return journey.

"What did you find out, Lofty?"

"Quite a lot."

"Such as?"

"I can't tell you, its all hush-hush!"

"Hush-hush my arse," said Scouse.

"What's so bloody important about a caravan?" queried Geordie.

"Listen, I'm sworn to secrecy, but between us three, I can tell you that it's for someone very high up."

Into view came the River Jordan, rushing and tumbling in haste as it neared the Dead Sea. Over the Allenby Bridge into Palestine. Conversation dries up, rifles made ready, on the alert. Three pairs of eyes narrowed by the glare of the sun, scan the road ahead, either side and beyond. Pass by Jericho. Mile after mile with not a soul in sight, we relax a little.

"Watch out, 200 yards at 10 o'clock!" My foot slammed down on the accelerator at Geordie's sudden shout. False alarm; over there to the left the blistering heat was playing its tricks. Despite our spell of rest and relaxation in Transjordan, our nerves were jangling.

"That tightened my arse up!" rasped Scouse.

"Same here," added Geordie and myself in unison.

Through Jerusalem, to the crossroads at Nathanya and into the comforting presence of the Kings Dragoon Guards and fellow gunners at Camp 21.

"I thought you'd gone AWOL, where've you been, Trev?" asked Bill Wilson as I braked to a halt.

"My lips are sealed, Bill."

"That's a change, anyway. Welcome back!"

After the 163 miles non-stop journey it was nice to sit back and unwind. We remained in the cab of the truck and smoked our cigarettes. Scouse started pumping me again. "Have you been in Transjordan before, Lofty?"

"Let's just say that I know some of those Arab Legion blokes almost as well as I know you!" "Bullshit!" said Geordie, entering into the discussion. "Are you going to tell us what this mission has been about or aren't you?"

"Some time soon, we are all going on a big scheme in Transjordan. Among other things we are to have the honour of firing a Royal Salute for King Abdullah."

"Bollocks!" they said as one. So much for telling the truth! Stretched out on my bed turning the day's events over in my mind, I wonder why I see the Galilean when I exit Palestine but never when I enter? Earlier today as I drove over the bridge at the border I'd snatched a quick look down but all I had seen was the turbulent water of the River Jordan.

A lively tune came into my head. I was at the home of my grandparents on my father's side. Ivy Farm House at Little Hucklow was full of relatives, some from as far away as the West Country. After the greetings came a few moments of solemn silence in remembrance of my Uncle Gerald, killed in action near Ypres in 1917. After refreshments and a lot of talking, out came Grandfather's cello and everyone stood and sang along with him as he played hymn after hymn. All of them had good voices, especially Aunt Lil and my dad. The singing always ended with a hymn about the River Jordan, the sacred river I had crossed that very morning.

"Shall we gather at the river, where higher angel feet have trod," I sang softly.

"Going all religious, Trev?" asked Slim.

"No, I was just trying to remember a hymn I last heard when I was a very small boy."

"Carry on, I was enjoying it," he said, closing his eyes, but by now my thoughts had moved on.

Sat in my Sunday best in Little Hucklow Chapel. Wedged between my older brother Noel and old Mrs Hallam. It wasn't incense that pervaded the air but the homely chapel scent I was used to. A peculiar but not unpleasant blend of furniture polish, mints, mothballs and 'Devon Violets.' Bigger and stronger than me, Noel pressed me up harder and harder against Mrs Hallam. She must have thought I was seeking comfort, for the tighter the squeeze the more she smiled at me. I felt I was in danger of being cuddled or kissed. I kicked him, which eased the pressure and brought a shout at the same time.

"That's naughty, Trevor!" exclaimed Mrs Hallam in a loud voice. Heads turned and from up front where he was waiting to sing his solo, dad glared at me. By the side of him the preacher kept droning on. "Behave yourself, Trevor," said mum in a loud whisper.

"It's not my fault, it's our Noel, he keeps on 'utching me up!"

A girl with ribbons in her hair leaned forward to look round my mum to see what was going off. I pulled a face at her, she started crying and near her a baby in arms joined in.

"You'll catch it, my lad, when you get home!" came the whispered assurance from mum. The moments of distraction near the end of his sermon caused the preacher to raise his voice; "Sodom," he shouted.

I sat up with a jerk; it was the second time I'd heard that expression within the hour. Before entering the chapel I had stood with Noel and mum as she talked with Mrs Francis, Mrs Middleton, and Mrs Hallam. "Owd 'em, Turn 'em!" came the shout. Nobody moved as half a dozen wild eyed sheep shot past. "Sod 'em! Let 'em goo!" came the exasperated cry from the red- faced farmer following on behind.

"Six days shalt thou labour. Today is the Lord's Day," said Mrs Hallam. "Shame," said Mrs Francis. Mrs Middleton stood tall and gave him a withering look. "Sorry, ladies," muttered the farmer as he hobbled past with downcast eyes.

"Gomorrah," continued the preacher in a loud voice. "Sodom and Gomorrah paid the penalty for their wickedness when the Lord rained brimstone and fire upon them, and destroyed them, and those who dwelled in them, and everything that grew there."

Today my eyes had followed the flow of the River Jordan to the Dead Sea and the salt flats to the south, where Lot's wife was transformed into a pillar of salt for looking back at Sodom. I think of the preacher's Sodom and the farmer's 'Sod 'em' spelt differently but sounding the same. Onward past Jericho where at the time my mind had been otherwise occupied. Now as I think of Jericho, the Derbyshire village of Foolow comes to mind, with its village green and Bulls Head pub set amidst the trees. Its pond complete with ducks and geese from Ollerenshaw's farm, waddling to and fro. Sturdy cottages, stately hall, gritstone cross, church and chapel. All of it encompassed by fields of different greens, picked out in squares and crazy shapes by the grey of limestone walls. This was a Sunday when Foolow's Wesleyan Reform Chapel was full to capacity. The congregation consisted largely of housewives, miners, quarrymen and farmers. The part-time preacher was also the postman who delivered their letters, six days a week.

His sermon about Joshua and Jericho was a familiar one. He went on at some length. It was hot and a trifle stuffy in the chapel. The congregation had dined well. Far better orators than Tammy would have had difficulty holding their undivided attention. Yawns became more frequent, eyes were closing, some were nodding off. Like other such part-time preachers, he expected no earthly rewards, but it would be nice if tomorrow, when he came with the post someone said "You did well Tammy!"

On the other hand, he was well aware that unless he regained their interest they would never let him forget how his sermon had put them to sleep. At Tammy's 'Jericho' the priests had already blown their trumpets six times, at Foolow the eyelids weighed heavy and continued to close. With his mind on rams-horn trumpets, Tammy seized on the fact that the rams in this locality either had small horns or none at all. A snore from the back triggered his excitement. Abandoning his written notes he shouted out, "Seven trumpets made from the horns of rams and they werna them little buggers!"

Those that were lolling sat bolt upright, some had grins on their faces. Flushed of face, Tammy cleared his throat and bravely carried on to the end of his sermon, "And Joshua's fame was noised throughout all the country."

"Amen."

And through a slip of the tongue, this congregation which included some from Eyam, Hucklow, Wardlow and Tideswell would noise Tammy's fame for years to come.

Through the Wilderness, where the only movement apart from our own had been a dancing mirage on shifting sand. Desolate and seemingly devoid of all life, yet in spring a miracle will carpet it with bright coloured flowers and life aplenty will follow. Enough at Jerusalem to occupy my thoughts for hours on end, but it's history and all it has to offer is overshadowed by knowledge of recent events. Atrocities by Jewish terrorists, who killed and wounded over a hundred people when they blew up part of the King David Hotel last year and who in March of this year blew up the Officers Club killing and wounding 29.

After Jerusalem, familiar ground for mile after mile. Place names pass by. Cavalrymen in their armour, Red Caps in jeeps. Artillerymen and infantrymen on foot patrols and in Bren-gun pits.

All that comes to mind now and to journeys end are everyday things that make up the routine demands of Internal Security Duties.

Chapter 14

More Thoughts of Home

November days pass slowly. During my time off, when I'm not catching up on lost sleep, I try to rid myself of the despondency that comes in on the wings of danger and monotony, and affects me from time to time.

Above in the clear blue sky the sun shines hot, I think of home but freezing fog comes to mind. I look across to the camp perimeter and the orange grove outside where the trees are mottled green. In the plantation in Tideswell's Townhead where I played as a boy, the trees which I climbed will have shed their dead leaves. From the branches of sycamore and ash came our bows and arrows, our staves and spears. Trunks with indiscriminate scars where sheath knives dug deep to make the sap weep as initials were carved. No hearts entwined, just TH BG GW CF ES. Three of us now in the Army and two of us in the Navy.

On the gentle breeze from the direction of the shimmering eucalyptus trees comes the acrid smell of wood smoke. It stirs memories within me of the Townhead bonfires on the moor. They will have held their bonfire two weeks ago. I try to visualise the Guy-topped fire and the people around it, but all I see is ashes in a large untidy circle of blackened earth. In vain I lick my lips to taste again home made treacle toffee and parkin. I have to settle for a brackish drink from my army water bottle. A look at photos of my loved ones should lift my spirits. I reached for the black leather wallet that held my treasured possessions. Faint now the ingrained stains of Hollebeke mud, but in their drab greyness still able to capture my thoughts of a war at a time before I was born. The wallet belonged to my Uncle Gerald, aged 19, killed in action with the 122nd Coy, Machine Gun Corps (Infantry) August 6th 1917. His wallet I hold in my hand is all that was found of him. His name is one of the 56,000 on the Menin Gate Hall of Memory who fell in the Ypres Salient and have no known grave. As a small boy I couldn't understand why his name was not on the Tideswell Cenotaph, then I found out that Little Hucklow was in Bradwell Parish.

Unbeknown to my parents I biked down to the Hope Valley to see his name on Bradwell War Memorial. On my way back, urged on by a thunderstorm I tried to pedal up steep Windmill Hill and my bike chain broke. With bloodied knees, a sprained wrist and home two and a half wet miles away, it was a day that comes readily to mind!

Friday, and as I prepared for another 24-hour spell of guard duties I say to myself, "I shall be bloody glad when it's Sunday" and for the first time in ages I laugh. I was 15 years of age at the time and working on the CWS coal lorry. A snowy Saturday morning in the village of Litton and the hundredweight bag of best Wingfield cobbles on my back weighed heavy. "You look tired out, Trevor lad!" remarked Mrs Redfern.

"Yes, I'm ready for a rest. I shall be glad when it's Sunday."

Mrs Redfern smiled and proceeded to tell me about two local ladies who worked at Cressbrook Mill. Housewives both, they were up and doing at 5 am for six days a week. After seeing to their husbands' and children's needs they had a two-mile walk to the mill. Long hours of drudgery amid bobbins, cotton dust and clattering machinery. After clocking off, they had a two-mile walk back home, most of which was uphill. On arrival they had meals to prepare and housework to do before they could call it a day. They were almost at the end of their working week at the Mill.

"Eh Polly, ah sholl be glad when it's Sunday"

"Ah dare na think o' Sunday, Clara, it's ter soon Monday again!"

Chapter 15

Battle in the Brewery

The terrorists haven't gone away. Beigin hasn't been captured. Illegal Jewish immigrants continue to arrive and continue to be transhipped. With every passing day, Arab resentment grows.

Another donkey in the orange grove, up against the perimeter wire, enjoying its moments of freedom in the dappled shade. The only semblance of shine on its dust covered coat were the dark sweat marks on its withers and the angry red weals on its flanks. Along its back ran the mark of a cross in a darker shade of hair.

I reported the animal's presence and back in the guardroom I asked if all donkeys bore such a mark. Nobody seemed to know nor care. Claimed by its owner, the donkey was gone before nightfall.

Some weeks back, a donkey in the same grove had neared the perimeter late at night during the hours of darkness. In the nearby Bren pit, 'Lofty' Rendle having received no response to his challenge opened up with the Bren. Thirty yards away the other Bren gun joined in. The poor beast never knew what hit it. The Arab owner got his compensation.

When I came off duty I sought out Lofty Rendle. "That donkey you shot, did it have the mark of a cross on its back"?

"I don't know, I never saw it, but Torquay donkeys and those I've ridden since, all did. After a moment's pause he asked with a grin, "Don't you have donkeys in the wilds of Derbyshire?"

"Not where I live."

"What about the scores of donkeys we see every day around here?"

"They're either toting something on their backs or wearing harness, pulling loads."

Lofty nodded and added "and all of them overworked."

This land takes my mind down strange roads. It seems fitting that the ass, so often ridiculed and ill treated, should bear the mark of a cross, 'the emblem of suffering and shame.' When I think of the ass I think of Jesus and His crown of thorns.

November ends with an upsurge of unrest at the news that the vote for the Partition of Palestine has been carried. After a couple of days it becomes clear to us that the Jews are happier than the Arabs with the decision of the United Nations.

Jewish hate towards us has not diminished, nor have their terrorist actions lessened. The spark of friendship the Arabs had for us has been extinguished by UNO's decision. Our situation can only get worse. Three days into December and it comes as no surprise when we hear reports of Arabs firing on British troops. I write home and tell them about the weather and the biblical places I've seen. I keep them informed about my mates and characters like Violets and Phantom.

Two weeks to another Christmas and I wonder how many more will pass before peace comes to this land. Despite everything I am beginning to look forward to the festivities. Two of the Danish lads provided my armed escort when I drove out of camp to fetch supplies. Big lads these Danes and well liked by all of us. They had joined the British Army expecting, like many of us, to fight the Axis Powers and finished up here, combating terrorists.

Bad news at the depot, no beer! "I daren't go back without beer, it's the only thing the lads have to look forward to!" "If you want it that bad, you'll have to fetch it from the brewery!"

With a signed and stamped chit in my pocket I followed the directions. After a surprisingly quiet journey we arrived at the ornamental iron gates fronting a large modern building on the coast near Jaffa.

The crack of a rifle, much too close for comfort, caused the Dane who was in the process of dismounting to change his mind. Three more shots in rapid succession, coming from atop the flat roofed houses just behind us, "You're OK to open the gates, it's the Arabs, they aren't aiming at us, they're shooting at the Jews in the Brewery!" Nobody moved, the firing increased. "We can't sit here," I thought. "If the Jews return the fire we are going to be caught in the middle." I decided to open the gates myself but my door wouldn't open. Twice, I put my shoulder to it, to no avail. I couldn't understand it.

"There is much danger, stay where you are, my friend!" the voice of the 'Galilean,' a voice that judging by their wide-eyed but unaltered expressions, had gone unheard by the two Danes. "Don't worry!" For a moment I almost added "the Galilean will protect us," but I thought better of it. "You there!" blasted the voice over the megaphone. I looked to my right, back up the road we had come down.

"Yes, you!"

I could see the Palestine policeman's head protruding out of the top of an armoured car. Oh, what a wonderful sight, I knew who was responsible for his arrival, it wasn't just luck!

"Do not get out, keep your doors shut and reverse back here!"

No sooner said than done. I greeted him with a smile which he didn't appreciate.

"What the bloody hell do you think you are doing?"

Silently, I wondered that myself. Risking the lives of the Danes and my own, for the sake of beer and me a 'Rechabite' since birth!

"Damn it, don't you know this area is out of bounds?"

His rank was no higher than mine, but calling him sir, I reasoned, would do no harm.

"Sorry sir, but the depot directed me here," I said, showing him the chit.

"Notices everywhere," he fumed. "Can't you bloody well read?"

"Yes officer, but I was concentrating on my driving and watching out for trouble."

"Can't your bloody escort read?"

"They're Danish and only know a smattering of English."

"Always an answer for everything, I've met clever buggers like you before. Let's have your details, starting with name, rank and number!"

"Do you know Graham Moulson?" I asked in desperation. He looked up from his notepad. 'I've only made matters worse,' I thought. Then I saw his expression change. "Yes, I know a Graham Moulson. If I remember correctly, he joined us on a transfer from the army in 1945."

"That's him, he comes from Cressbrook, we've known each other since we were lads."

"What a small world!" he said putting away his notepad and pencil.

"Is Graham stationed with you?" I asked.

"No, he was with me at Nablus, then I think he went to Bethlehem, hang on a minute." He said and ducked down into his armoured car. After a brief conversation with his companions he reappeared, "At present, Graham's stationed at Jenin."

"Thanks. If I get a chance I'll look him up next time I'm in that area. When you see him, tell him Trevor Hall has been asking about him."

"Trevor Hall," he repeated. "I remember Graham telling me about a cousin of his in the Army called 'Tiny' Hall, who he met up with in Haifa."

"That would have been Ken Hall, a giant of a man from Litton. I know him well, in fact I worked with his younger brother Roy on the Co-op bread van before I enlisted."

Nearby, the rifle fire of the Arabs was still meeting with no response from the Jews. I decided to press my luck, "I don't suppose its in your power to let me pick up a few crates of ale before I go?"

A frown puckered his brow. "Half an hour at the most," I urged.

"Half an hour and not a minute longer!" he said pointing up the side road that lead to the rear of the building.

"Take the coast road out, it should be quieter. In future keep away from 'Out of bounds' areas and if the Military Police get you we haven't seen you, understand?"

"OK and thanks a lot."

"We are in a hurry," I said handing over the depot chit to an oldish man in a khaki dustcoat. He nodded and shouted out instructions in a language I didn't understand.

"Help yourselves to a few drinks," said the young Jew in perfect English. There were 12 bottles in the crate he had brought us. Such was the heat, I was on my third bottle before I even tasted it and the Danes were ahead of me!

In 25 minutes the lorry was loaded and we were ready to go. "Can we ride with you to our homes just along the road," the young Jew asked, shoving more bottles of beer in the cab for us. "OK, but hurry up and keep out of sight!" I watched them climb aboard and I realised that we had more Jews in the back than we had crates of beer.

'Stay where you are, armoured car,' I said to myself, waving to the policeman at the bottom of the road.

Along the bumpy track by the coast, it dawned on me why my passengers were so keen to obtain a ride. For a few hundred yards it was open ground exposed to the Arab snipers on the flat-roofed houses. Thankfully, no bullets came our way.

As soon as I braked to a stop, the brewery workers were away running towards the cluster of houses without a word of thanks or goodbye.

At the nearby junction where we joined a tarmacadam road, a white robed figure raised a hand, I waved back. The Danish lads were looking at me as if waiting for an explanation. I said nothing. Not a word was spoken by any of us until we reached Camp 21.

"Say nothing to nobody about going into the out-of-bounds area, otherwise we shall all get it in the neck!" I made sure they understood before we unloaded.

"Lights out," and here in Kfar Yona all is quiet. Not all those Jews I've seen and met today will be asleep just yet. Some among them under the cloak of darkness have mines to lay, traps to set and triggers to squeeze, and all of us who wear the King's uniform are their targets. After a time the unseen enemy causes the mind to run riot and jumping at my own shadow is a common occurrence. Thank God for the Galilean who keeps me safe and sane.

With the last bottle of my free beer, I drank a toast to my good fortune of knowing a Cressbrook lad in the Palestine Police. "Graham Moulson, your very good health!"

Chapter 16

Christmas 1947

Later than usual I posted my Christmas cards. A few pictured Bethlehem and Nazareth but most of them were 6th Field RA Regimental cards, depicting the badges of the 'Rocket,' 'Eagle' and 'Dragon' Troops. Very smart and colourful but not very Christmassy.

"Any lumberjacks among you?"

I had done quite a bit of sawing and chopping before my call-up. I had also courted a couple of the Tideswell-based Timber Corps girls who worked in the woods near Sparrowpit.

"Yes, sergeant." I said, coming to attention.

"Fall out and report to the QM."

I was expecting to draw from the quartermaster's store a saw and an axe to do a bit of felling. Perhaps over there, for the proximity of orange and eucalyptus trees to the camp perimeter and the cover they offered to terrorists was obvious. Wherever the trees wanted felling, it should provide a welcome change from my present onerous duties.

"I'm the lumberjack that's required, 'Q'!"

"Hall, isn't it?" and without waiting for an answer he said with a smile on his face, "This way." With sinking heart I followed him into a large tent and arrived at the wood, an untidy, dusty great pile of it.

"When you've cleaned 'em all up, lay out on this side all the undamaged tent poles, pegs and miscellaneous items in their respective groups. On the other side, do the same with any that are damaged."

"It's going to take a long while, 'Q,' can you get me off my usual duties for a few days or so?"

"No! just keep at it in your time off. There's no rush, so long as it's all ship shape by Saturday." Considering today was Thursday, I decided to get on with it. I think my volunteering days are over.

At Christmas time in the Holy Land the terrorists continue to exact their remorseless toll of British lives. Bloodshed between Arab and Jew is on the increase. Duties are as normal, but dinner is better than usual and with it comes a present of two bottles of beer.

'Neath the garlands and balloons the officers wait on us. We sing a carol, I think of home, of peace and goodwill and red breasted robins in the snow. When I sang carols as a boy I used to think of Jesus and Bethlehem, of shepherds and wise men.

I think of the Methodist preachers and Sunday School teachers of my childhood. If God was boring at times, he also made me smile. If he frightened me he also comforted me. He understood and forgave me. I think of the kindly Rev. Thomas, minister of the Congregational

Church at the 'top o' the lane' and the ever-so-gentle Rev. Clegg before him. Of priests and vicars I cannot speak, but I know that in all of Tideswell's five different places of worship can be found compassion, friendship and help.

All to soon it is time to take up my rifle again. I 'stand to,' wondering why in the Holy Land, of all places, is there so much ungodliness and at the same time so much religious fervour?'

A letter from home informed me that dad was keeping cheerful despite his incapacity due to the illness that had struck him down around the time of my call-up. Everyone else was keeping well. Mum, along with June and Peter, had been over to Peak Forest to the family graves. Next to the grave of my grandfather Critchlow, who died after breaking his back through falling off a cartload of hay, lie my brother and sister, Gerald and Marjorie, who died in their infancy. All three had died before I was born. Marjorie and Gerald's coffins had cost one pound, eight shillings each. I had found the paid bill on the wire hook, where mum kept all her receipts.

Peak Forest, nestling round a wooded hill situated midway between Tideswell and Chapel-en-le-Frith. Farmsteads and cottages, cricket field, Reading Room and School. 'Devonshire Arms,' where from a nearby bonfire I salvaged a document which lies in my treasure chest, far away in Tideswell's Townhead. I can recall its every detail:

Belfast	March 1895
Mr William Hill	
Peak Forest	
Dr 839	To Dunville & Co Limited
To 29¼ Galls. Irish Whisky @ 4/=	5–17–0
To Duty on same	19- 6–1
	£25–3-1
April 9th By Cash	
Dunville & Co	
(Signed over)	A. Reid.
(a one penny stamp)	9–4-95

Across the road a church, High Peak's own 'Gretna Green,' where until 1804 clandestine weddings were held. On the corner a Co-op shop, managed by my Uncle Jack. At the far end, Uncle Sam's Smithy, tucked away where the road leads to Boggart Hole Lane. An expanse of water and near the Old Dam, the homes of my relatives. Nearby, the Methodist Chapel, hub and gathering place for the Critchlows.' To weddings, funerals and sermons, from the moors of Tideswell and Bradwell. From Poynton Cross and Waterfall over Fodew way. From farm and cottage on the heath near Smalldale. From Edale by Shivering

Mountain and Perryfoot.

I read the rest of mum's letter and smiled at the postscript Noel had added: "Watch out for them Philistines!"

Sister June and Brother Peter hadn't yet been born and I was still in short trousers. It was Sunday and the weather was set fair. Mum, Aunt Sarah, my older brother Noel and myself set off with Uncle Colin in his pony-drawn trap on the 4½ miles journey to Peak Forest. Up Townhead Moor, along grassy lanes past 'Silver Hillocks,' down to 'Brook Bottom' near 'Dropping Tor' with its watercress and sticklebacks. We followed the brook almost to its source. At the Guidepost we turned left over the moor by Potluck and Pittlemere to the old Peak Tavern, now Mount Pleasant Farm, the home of Aunt Jane and Uncle Stephen. Down past the opening of Boggart Hole Lane. Visible on the hillside to the north, the Bottomless Hole and hidden away over the hill, Winnats Pass, eerie places that gives me the shivers. "Steady, Belle," Uncle Colin's reassuring voice calmed the pony as its hooves slipped every now and then on the shiny tarmac on the steep downward bends of the Mount leading to the village half a mile below. Once on the level, the few hundred yards to the Chapel was taken at a brisk trot.

After we had dismounted, Uncle Colin had a few quick words with everyone present and then went off to see to Belle and spend some time with Uncle Sam.

The service wasn't due to start for almost an hour. Noel and myself stood while people kissed us, patted us and remarked on how we had grown. Most of the men were smoking strong twist in pipes that bubbled and sizzled. The women were talking hats, most of which had been purchased in Buxton. I heard Milligans mentioned. My Mum's and Aunt Sarah's hats were Beatty Bramwell's finest from her Tideswell High Street shop.

Called in by the notes of the organ, my heart sank when I saw the preacher was the one from over Dove Holes way who could talk for hours on end. It was hot in the crowded chapel. When the preacher finally arrived at his sermon my mind was already wandering. He started on about David and Goliath. I'd heard it all before.

I counted the imitation cherries on the organist's hat and spent several minutes adding them up with the hymn numbers on the board. "One thousand, six hundred and sixteen," I whispered to Noel, but he took no notice. Mum frowned at me and shook her head.

In the row in front, the blue-green feathers that adorned Aunt Mary's hat caught my attention. They reminded me of the sapphire flash of kingfishers at Water-cum-Jolly. My thoughts drifted to the river, where fat trout wait to be tickled and where, three of us once bathed without any clothes. With an almost imperceptible puff of my cheeks, I caused Aunt Mary's feathers to shiver and shimmer, but she felt the air on her neck and turned round.

"Behave yourself!" whispered Mum. From shivering feathers, my mind turned to nearby Castleton's Shivering Mountain, which on the maps is called 'Mam Tor.' I was thinking "It isn't really a mountain, but then, neither is the one we've come down today into Peak Forest. It was at this point that I heard a shout: "The Philistines are on yonder Mount!"

Startled, I jumped up and looked towards the Mount, then I realised where I was and, hot of cheeks, I sat down quickly. Mum cleared her throat and gave a deep sigh. Noel and cousin Vernon were grinning at me and after a fair bit of muttering and shuffling amongst the congregation, the preacher raised his hand aloft and returned to the Valley of Elah.

After the service was over there was a lot of talking to be done before the gathering went their different ways. Aunt Jane was the only one to mention the disturbance in the Chapel. "Your Trevor jumped up quick during the sermon, did something sting him?"

"No, my trousers were cutting into me, they're too tight they're our Noel's old cast offs," I said before Mum could answer.

"Your trousers are almost new," retorted Mum and turning to Aunt Jane said: "Noel had hardly worn them before he'd grown out of them."

"We noticed your new net curtains when we came past, did you get them in Buxton?" asked Aunt Sarah changing the subject.

"No, I got them from Manchester."

It was curtains and dresses and hats yet again. Almost an hour later the goodbyes had been said, we were on our way. We looked back and waved as we turned left on to the main road. "Gid up, Belle," we passed by the Devonshire Arms at a brisk trot.

I listened to Mum and Aunt Sarah talk about Aunt Grace's and Aunt Rhoda's hats. When they began discussing 'Our Poll' I knew they were referring to Aunt Mary, but why do they call her 'Poll'? And Aunt Polly at White Rake Farm, is she really Polly or another Mary? I'll ask them when I can get a word in.

We started the long climb up the Mount.

"Watch out up here Uncle Colin!"

"Why, Noel?" he asked rather anxiously.

"There's some Philistines about!"

I kicked Noel's shin, he kicked me back.

"Stop the trap please, Colin."

"Get out the pair of you. Noel you walk up front near the pony's head; Trevor you walk behind the trap."

"Gid up, Belle," the trap got on the move again.

"What's all the trouble about, Emily?" asked Uncle Colin.

"It's our Trevor again, he was daydreaming while the sermon was on, and the preacher shouted out that the Philistines were on the Mount and it made him jump."

"He jumped up and looked through the window!" Noel called out from up front.

"You're a liar!" I shouted from the back.

"That's enough from both of you and on the Sabbath as well. Just you wait till your Dad hears about it!"

Chapter 17

Going Home

January 1st 1948.

Thirteen more days to go and, God willing, I should be on my way home for demobilisation.

Daily the situation here in Palestine continues to worsen. North of Haifa, an illegal Jewish immigrant ship has avoided detection and landed her human cargo. Here in Nathanya, well over a hundred illegal Jewish immigrants have been found and arrested. Up and down the land the killing and wounding goes on.

On January 6th, watched by Slim, I crossed another day off my calendar.

"A week tomorrow, Trev you'll be heading back to the Derbyshire hills!" he remarked.

"Hopefully!" I replied.

Next morning at breakfast, Phantom paused by our table. "I've just learned from one of the RHQ wallahs that we are now with the 1st Guards Brigade in Divisional Reserve."

"What does that mean?" inquired 'Scouse.'

"Fuck knows!" replied 'Phantom,' and off he went.

There are no noticeable changes. Our way of life remains the same. The days come and go.

"Stand to!" This time it's a false alarm.

"Stand down!"

Another night has passed, another morale-sapping guard duty is over. It should be my last one. I crossed another day off, only two to go.

"Any snow up your way yet, Trev?" asked Hursty as I read my newly-arrived letter from home. "Just a skittering, according to my mum." I replied.

Enclosed in her letter was a leaflet. "Your Uncle Tom Critchlow from Berrystall Lodge on Bradwell Moor, has sent you this to remind you of home," she had written at the bottom. It was a single folded page printed by; Ernest Elliot, Bradwell. Entitled "Owd Bradda Hasna Had It Yet." A local poet tells how Bradwell fared during the great snow-up. Threepence Each. Proceeds for Men's Effort Easter. 1947.

I found the poem to be very interesting and amusing.

"Are you going to share what you are laughing at with us?" enquired Slim as I began to read through for the third time.

"It's a local thing and some of it is in dialect. You need to know the area and the people, to really appreciate it." I told him.

"Just read it out, I'll go to sleep if I don't like it!" he replied.

"Go on, Trev, get on with it," urged Hursty.

"Right then, pin your ears back and no interruptions!"

Well, folk, how are you liking th' storm,
How are yo' fixed for coal,
An how's th'owd chilblains getting on,
Are awe yor limbs still whole?
Folk talk about th'awd - fashioned storms
They had in days of yore,
Eh dear! If this is one o'them,
I hope to see no more.
I'd like to sing the praise of aw
Who helped us thro' those days,
For those brave men and women too
Deserve our highest praise.
When th' New Nook lay engulfed in snow,
One farmer proved a brick,
For neither blinding snow nor drift
Could stop the Clarence "click."
We heard that aw'd familiar "click"
Above the raging wind,
Then Clarence and his sledge appeared
Wi milk for aw mankind.
George Andrew with his yead lapt up,
Fra' th' Within ploughed a track,
He meant to serve his customers
Or break th' awd chestnut's back.
An' how they get fra' Berrystall
Nobody'll ever know,
I'm sure Miss Critchlow must ha' trudged
Up to her neck I' snow.
Joe Wilson and his bonny lass
Just ploughed their way fra' Brough
Thro' th' snow in Stretfield lay yards deep,
Th' Green Van must do its stuff.
And Willoughby joined in the fight,
He didna sit a' whom,
He'd one advantage over Joe,
He'd non as far to come.
To try and get to Hartle Moor
Folk said wor just a joke,
But Cyril Braddu bravely went
And browt th' milk down for folk.
King David was no braver mon
When he faced th' Philistines,

Than David who fra' Hazelbadge
Took th' milk to th' railway lines.
Our bakers didna let us down,
When outside transport stopped,
They turned out mony a hundred loaves,
An' baked until they dropped.
And Eales with his brave little lads
Browt th' papers night an morn.
I'll bet that mony a time they wished
That they had ne'er been born.
And Rowland with his gallant staff
Achieved what they strove for
Brave Jack and Mary climbed the heights
Crying "Excelsior."
When brave Lol landed with his stuff
The queue stretched for miles they say,
I'm sure kind - hearted Mrs Firth
Saved mony lives that day.
Some stood wi' faces black and blue,
They say some nearly died,
Some stuck it to th' bitter end
A few went whom and cried.
John Middleton and Alfie tramped
O'er th' moors their sheep to reach
For what they went through these brave chaps
Deserve a medal each
Why Merlin ever tried to get through
I'm sure I dunno know,
Why did he slide fra' Paradise
Into this vale of woe.
Sometimes I tak' a walk up the Rake
To friends at th' Lordship Farm,
I wonder if they're living yet
I hope they've ta'en no harm.
Beneath Great Hucklow's alpine shroud
"Othello" lies in sleep,
While play and players, empty stalls
Their anxious vigils keep.
The play's the thing so Shakespeare said,
And so the bards all sing,
But up i th' Peak o' Derbyshire
Just now the Snow's the thing.
It's grand to see th' awd Pensioners
Each Friday on the job,

Pidpodding' through the snow to fetch
Their six and twenty bob.
An' I'm sure th' angels up above
Now sing a sweeter song,
When they look down and see th' awd folk
Go toddlin' along.
"You've had it" is a common phrase
Yo' often hear today,
But Bradda hasna' "had it" yet,
An' never will, I say.
Tho' storms may rage and fires dee out,
An' th' electric leet be gone,
While we've a 'lulo and a cow,
Owd Bradda 'll carry on.
So as we walk on top o' th' waws
An view the landscape o'er,
Let's think we're two yards nearer Heaven
Than we've e'er been before.

March 1947. I.M.H.

January13th 1948

Drawn my pay, had my medical, documentation all in order. Like all OR's I can have my full kit packed and be on the move to anywhere inside 10 minutes. My mates are all on duty, I have the tent to myself.

After checking the contents of my wallet, I spread the rest of my personal possessions on the bed. Cigarettes, matches, coins, including a silver threepenny bit, francs and piastres. Two Army knives, a leaking fountain pen, an indelible pencil, some photos and a wad of useless large-denomination drachma notes, printed by the German Occupation forces in Greece.

"Hey up, Lofty Trev, is it right that you are going home?" asked Violets.

"Yes mate, I'm away tomorrow."

Looking serious, he sat down on the bed.

"Is something the matter?" I asked.

He nodded, "That young officer that's not been here long wanted to know what caused that big dent in the shithouse roof. I told him I didn't know."

"You should have said that it was a bolt from heaven."

"I would have if I'd thought of it. Anyway, he ordered me to make the roof good and whitewash it again before his next inspection. Well I tried to hammer the dent out but I've knocked a fucking big hole in the roof and the dent is now on the inside."

I burst out laughing and he laughed with me.

"When is the inspection due?"

He moved his lips silently before mouthing "Tomorrow." Then springing to his feet in panic he shouted, "Fucking hell, it's tomorrow!"

"Settle down, let's have a smoke while I think things through." As I held a match to his cigarette I noticed how thick his eyebrows had grown after being severely singed.

Once before he had come to me in desperation about the lavatories under his jurisdiction. They were infested with a plague of beetles, big and black. They made their home in the big circular pit beneath the wooden lavatory seats. When the sun went down the beetles came up and attached themselves to the posterior of anyone that sat down. Then as now, Violets was at his wits end, for the beetles seemed immune to all his disinfectants and poisons. With constipation rife and tempers short he was the target for much abuse.

He sought my help. I advised him to pour a drop of petrol into the pit, light a ball of paper, throw it in and run. Will it shift 'em?" he asked. I assured him it would.

It was an extremely hot afternoon, and as usual, all of us off duty were resting in the shade of the tents. From a distance of about 30 yards I watched Violets enter the 12-seater carrying a jerrican in each hand. If those cans were full, some 8 gallons of petrol was spicing up a 10-ton pudding of beetle-infested excreta. Petrol vapour and methane gas! My shout of warning was lost in the explosion. Up in the clear blue sky went a tin roof sheet, followed, caught up and passed by a fast growing cloud. Thinking it was a terrorist raid, naked men clutching rifles burst out of the canvas shelters. I was already running for safety and when their startled eyes took in the ominous cloud above, they followed me fast. A few tail enders got splattered and quite a few tents and whitewashed stones received a coat of khaki. Violets appeared out of the haze. Hatless and with his eyebrows and hair badly singed he had a grin on his face–"That's shifted the buggers, Trev!"

"Yes, and it's shifted us as well. I should keep out of the way for a while if I was you." But all that's in the past. Now he has another problem that needs solving.

" Have you thought of anything yet?" Violets asked anxiously.

I nodded, "Can you get any glue?"

"I've got some of that!"

"What about canvas?"

"No, I've none of that."

"You need a piece large enough to cover the dent. Cut a piece from one of the tents, but not ours."

"I daren't do that."

"Cut a piece out of some bugger's kitbag then, and stick it on to cover the dent and the hole, then coat it with very thick whitewash."

"You're a bloody genius," he said, slapping me on the back." I shall miss you, Trev."

"Before you go, Violets would you like one of these army knives?"

"No I've got two of them."

"A fountain pen?"

"I've got two of them."

"A pencil, dodgy drachma?"

"I've plenty of them buggers."

"Have you any of these? I asked, handing him a dog-eared collection of saucy photos given to me by Yorky before his demob."

Eyes widening all the time, he thumbed through them slowly. Each photo in turn was greeted with an expression of admiration accompanied by a laugh, a "bloody hell" or a "bugger me!"

"Stick 'em in your pocket, they're yours!"

"Thanks a lot mate, have a safe journey home, I've got your address, if I survive I'll look you up sometime."

I nodded. "Look after yourself Violets."

We shook hands and he scuttled off to get on with his roof repairs.

As I watched him disappear, I thought, there's little wonder that we value pornographic pictures so highly. Throughout this land, although well aware of the dangers and the need for concentration and caution there is much temptation. It is impossible not to notice the beauty of sun-tanned Jewish girls in revealing blouses and skimpy shorts.

'Don't touch,' 'off limits.' The unavailability of female contact or friendship makes for a monastic life and increases the voyeuristic traits in all of us.

We had only been back from the canteen for half an hour and already Slim, Frank and Hursty were fast asleep. I had brought half a dozen bottles of Gold Star with me, a couple each for Roy Herod and Jim Wiley who were out on duty and a couple for tomorrow's journey. I had spent far more than I had intended buying farewell drinks in the bar, but I had no regrets.

Try as I might, sleep wouldn't come to me. My mind was all over the place. I found myself thinking of the Romans who occupied this land at the time of Christ. I thought not of commanders but those under their command. Most of what I've learned about the Roman soldier has been derogatory, but in the absence of his voice, who can judge how fairly history has dealt with him? I recalled my first meeting with the Galilean. He spoke of a teacher who told the people the way to the Kingdom of Heaven. What the 'Galilean' went on to say about the teacher –

Since that time his words have been manipulated and his teachings distorted to comply with the desires of man and his institutions."

– has caused me to question things that previously I accepted without question.

The 'Galilean' himself, raises many questions within me. In vain, I try to push them from the forefront of my mind, for they are questions I don't want to contemplate while I'm within the confines of Palestine. I want to believe the 'Galilean' is real but there are times when such a belief doesn't make sense. If only he had a distinctive feature, if only he had a face. Those others he has spoken to, why don't they speak up? But there again, why don't I? "Some day I will!" I whispered to myself.

By torchlight I looked at my watch. Ten minutes after midnight, January 14th has arrived. I lit up a cigarette and poured myself a bottle of beer. I looked at my sleeping comrades and thought of others out there on duty. In a way I'm going to miss them. On each other our lives have depended and at such times, thank God, none of us have been found wanting. The bonds that bind us may loosen with time, but they will never break. I raised my tin mug and drank a silent toast 'to comradeship.'

Still wide-awake, I looked around for something to read. All I could find was a pocket Bible. "Plenty in this to put me to sleep," I reasoned as I focused my eyes on the very small print.

Tense as a coiled spring I opened my eyes. I sensed a presence and could hear faint sounds of movement. On the sand where it had fallen, my torch shone with the gleam of a battery almost spent. Slowly and silently I reached for the bayonet by my bedside. Suddenly I froze as I touched something warm, then I felt the rasp of a rough tongue licking my fingers. With much relief I realised it was Dog.

A flash of anger followed my relief. "Damn you, Dog, you frightened the life out of me." I muttered to myself. Obviously attracted by the smell of beer, the mongrel sat watching me as I picked up the torch along with my mug, which I noticed, had been licked clean. My watch showed I had been asleep for almost four hours. Until now, I'd forgotten all about Dog, who I hadn't seen for some time.

"I've known you ever since I first came to this land." He cocked his head on one side as though he knew what I was thinking. "You are highly honoured, Dog," I whispered as I poured the bottle of Gold Star earmarked for my journey home into the mug and placed it on the ground. Without a pause he lapped up the beer, then licking his lips he raised his head and looked at me as if expecting more. Reaching down for the empty mug I whispered harshly "Go on, bugger off, Dog, you've got what you came for!"

Never noted for showing affection, he surprised me when he rested his lame front leg on my hand and licked my face. Looking down into his sad rheumy eyes, I stroked his head and whispered softly, "Sorry, Dog, I do believe you've come to say goodbye"!

Chapter 18

Home At Last

Twenty-one years of age, I was now a man, with much to catch up on and much to do. In my life ahead there was no place for Palestine and its memories – or so I thought.

Here where I live, lightning's flash and thunder's clap are frequent visitors. Splitting open leaden skies, they come and dance and roll around as if imprisoned by the hills. As in the past, from nearby quarries the blasts still come to shake doors, rattle windows and tremble the ground beneath my feet.

None of these things bothered me before, but now the coming of each one makes me jump in some alarm. When I cross the moor, the sudden flight of a flushed bird and the springing up of a startled hare, the sights of which once gave me joy, now makes me catch my breath and tighten up. In night's darkness, the snap of a rotten twig underfoot, fingers me with a moment's fright that sets my heart pounding.

Eventually with the help of 'time, the great healer' and a couple of bottles of "Easton's Syrup" from the local chemist, my jumpiness – my legacy of Palestine, departed.

Then in an unstable world with another war looming, my country required my services again. For a brief period I was called up as a 'Z reservist.' Once more under canvas but this time on Salisbury Plain. They made sure that I was fit and still knew how to fight, but with the training and the gunfire came back memories, as the Army brought me up to scratch.

Year upon year, rarely is Israel – the country I knew as Palestine – out of the news.

We parted as young men; we met again as pensioners. 'Slim' Horridge had been with me at Galilee, I could talk to him about 'that day,' but as in 1946, I said nothing.

In 1997 the formation of the Palestine Pals Association and the dawning of a new Millennium made me resolve to relate my memories of Palestine and in doing so fulfil a promise I made over half a century ago.

Thinking back over that time I realised how apt were the words from the 44th Chapter of the Book of Ecclesiastes:

"And some there be which have no memorial, who are perished as though they had never been; and are become as though they had never been born"

From the attic I fetched a large brown envelope that had gathered dust and cobwebs. I emptied out the contents which hadn't seen the light of day since my demobilisation. On unfolding a much fingered route card a few grains of sand fell out – Palestinian or Transjordanian I wondered?

Stuck to a 156 Transit Camp's receipt for a rifle and 50 rounds of ammunition were the scribbled directions to the 'Gold Star' brewery at Jaffa.

Yellow with age, the *Mail* picture and report of the illegal immigrant ship *San Dimitrio* held my attention for a few moments.

I didn't dwell on the copy of the *Daily Express* dated August 1st 1947. I needed neither pictures nor the front-page headlines – "HANGED BRITONS: PICTURE THAT WILL SHOCK THE WORLD," to remind me of the atrocity and its perpetrators. On the topmost page of the bundle of notes I had made during my service in the Holy Land, I had written – "We continue to bury our dead with dreadful regularity – the military cemeteries are situated at Khayat Beach and Ramle. Note: Ramle is the reputed birthplace of St. George of England."

Lastly I opened a small envelope marked with a 'G' and read the notes within. At the times of happenings it had all seemed real enough. Shortly afterwards when writing it up I had harboured doubts. On leaving Palestine, those doubts had grown and been replaced with a belief and a certainty that my experiences with the 'Galilean' had been more to do with imagination than fact. Yet, more than anything else, it is the contents of the envelope marked 'G' that caused me to take up my pen.

Appendices

On May 14th 1948 the United Nations Mandate to Britain to govern Palestine was terminated. It had originally been granted by the League of Nations after Palestine was liberated from Turkish rule after the First World War by British and Anzac troops commanded by General Allenby.

Menachem Beigin, Commander of the "IRGUN ZVAI LEUMI," was neither captured nor brought to justice. Instead, he became Prime Minister of Israel on May 18th 1977. On October 27th 1978 he was awarded the NOBEL PEACE PRIZE.

In 1997 George Webb founded the "Palestine Pals Association" for ex-gunners who had served in Palestine 1945–48

In 1999 Gerry Burr and George Webb founded the "Palestine Veterans Association" for all members of the British Armed Services who served in Palestine 1945 - 48.

Gerry Burr arranged with Nick Hill (Archivist) for the dedication to Palestine of HUT No.13 at Eden Camp Modern History Theme Museum, MALTON, N. YORKS.

Veterans rallied to George and Gerry's call. £2,000 was raised for a Memorial stone, now erected in the Arboretum at ALREWAS.

On May 19th 2001 we came together again to remember our 784 comrades who fell in Palestine. 1945–48.

The Roll of Honour based on information supplied by the Commonwealth War Graves Commission was compiled by George Webb. The total of 784 does not include the losses sustained by the Palestine Police. It has been published in full by Arcturus Press, publishers of this present volume.

And their glory shall not be blotted out.
Their bodies are buried in peace;
But their name liveth for evermore.

(From the 44th Chapter of the Book of Ecclesiastes.)